The Beauty and Courage of Sudan

Why a Dream of Peace Is Possible

Mission Study

by Linda Beher

with *Study Guide*
by Maxine West

Handwritten notes:

Discrible Sudan
words:
   differences
   challenges
   complicated
   complexities
   difficult to understand
   diversity
   destablized

   displacement
   destruction
   masking
   struggle
   torn + bruised
   dream for peace by all
   hope

Map: p. 13
Facts: p 15

Women's Division • General Board of Global Ministries • The United Methodist Church

Photo Credits:
Paul Jeffrey/ACT-Caritas: front cover, pp. 2, 14, 16, 18, 22, 26, 36, 43, 45, 46, 48, 49, 59, 63, 70, 72, 79, 84, 86, 88, 90, 102, 122, 127, 144, 146
Paul Jeffrey/UMCOR: pp. 3, 4, 5, 7, 9

Michelle Scott/UMCOR: pp. 32, 34, 35

Courtesy of iStock Photo: pp. 10, 54, 96

The Beauty and Courage of Sudan: Why a Dream of Peace Is Possible
Copyright © 2009 Women's Division, The General Board of Global Ministries, The United Methodist Church
A publication of the Women's Division, The General Board of Global Ministries, The United Methodist Church

ISBN# 978-1-933663-33-3

Library of Congress Control Number: 2008943800

Printed in the United States of America.

Author's Acknowledgment

To the women and men of United Methodist Committee on Relief, serving in Sudan and some 80 other countries. Their courage, insight, and faith were the seeds of this book.

"More than anything, one is struck by the light."
—*Ryszard Kapuscinski*

Table of Contents

Introduction

The largest country in Africa, Sudan encompasses an area the size of the United States east of the Mississippi River. Once it declared independence from foreign rule in 1956, Sudan has been at war, for no easily described reasons. Economic, political, racial, religious, and cultural influences all played their part. As differences in these basic life areas stirred the winds of war, uncertain rains heightened the quarrel over resources—scores went hungry and thirst and violence escalated. All the protagonists in the various civil wars contributed to the ruin of crops and the disruption of subsistence farming throughout South Sudan and, later, throughout Darfur. In spite of peace accords, in 2008 war continued to affect the lives of tens of thousands in this ancient land.

At Khartoum the Blue and White Niles converge into one great river flowing north. Pyramids predating the Egyptian structures at Luxor push up from the Nubian Desert at Merowe, north of Khartoum. The road leading away from the capital to the antique burial grounds is paved; 130 miles of the approximately 2,684 miles of paved roads in the country. The story of this frontier country is more complex and ambiguous than many Westerners—those of us living outside Africa—can imagine.

For most of the past twenty years Sudan has been plagued with severe drought. Desertification is apparent in the West, where thorn bushes dominate the savanna landscape of South Darfur and are destroying the native shrubbery like acacia trees. The wadis, those watercourses that swell and shrink with seasonal rains, are often baked dry. The shortages of food due to drought have sometimes reached famine proportions. Climate change in Sudan is not just a looming crisis; it is the reality on the ground.

Yet at Sudan's core is beauty. Polish journalist Ryszard Kapuscinski captured it well: "More than anything, one is struck by the light." Along with the landscape's beauty, there is an interior beauty—the spirit of courage;

Local blacksmiths make hand tools such as rakes and hoes for farmers' use near El Ferdous, a displaced persons camp in South Darfur.

(Paul Jeffrey, UMCOR)

At a South Darfur displaced persons camp a builder creates a *rakouba*, or open-sided shelter, that he will finish with a woven roof. *Rakoubas* are commonly used for group meetings in camp.

(Paul Jeffrey, UMCOR)

a richness of tradition, antiquity, cultures, and natural resources; human interchange; and endurance in all its mystery. Sudan also contains a richness of contradictions. Its beauty contrasts with and suffers from the carnage and violence that has marked much of its long history. Sudan's many ethnicities and languages both enrich the culture and become touchpoints for conflict. Its conflicts have created shortages of everyday resources like food and water for the many—and have consolidated in the hands of a few the riches of oil from one of the world's largest oil basins. On an August morning in the streets of the capital, Khartoum, Mercedes-Benzes share the road with donkey carts and sheep drovers and the white SUVs of the nongovernmental organizations.

Every day except Friday, the day of prayers—and since 2008, Saturday, named by the Sudan Cabinet Council as a second weekend day—men and women of Khartoum head for their offices or the market. Businesswomen wear finely woven, embroidered white linen covers over their Western-style suits. Other women wear long black hijabs, as headscarves are called in Arabic, and veils, called *niqabs*, covering their faces. A few women add long black gloves for full coverage—only their eyes are visible. Army personnel, guns at the ready, speed along the shoulders of the road in open all-terrain vehicles. Music pulses from the *souks*, or street markets, and from the CD players in every car. People walk in the street; the sidewalks are broken, or missing altogether.

It is hot in this metropolis of 4 to 6 million people—40 C, or over 100 degrees—on an August day near the end of the rainy season in the North and the beginning of the annual dry season. Windows are open in offices and autos. A metallic weaving of bumpers, fenders, headlights, and hoods results when a traffic guide leaves his post for a break. There is a mall, with escalators, and across the street from that, men from the countryside in brown robes and head coverings, called *ema*, sell their sheep. There is a market for fresh lamb during Ramadan, the monthlong period each year when all Muslims fast during daylight hours.

Women at El Ferdous, a camp in South Darfur, build a *gotia*, or conical shelter, with grasses collected from the savanna. When finished, the *gotia* will house a family.
(Paul Jeffrey, UMCOR)

Contrasts cont.

Far away from Khartoum, to the West and to the South, contrasts continue. For instance, there are towns with unpaved, winding streets, little more than the tracks of camels or donkeys. Tall middens, or barriers of refuse and scraped sand, defy easy crossing by people on foot. A woman and child trek along on the back of a donkey, with small sticks of firewood loaded behind them. From a nearby camp farm, sounds of singing and drumming float over the dry air. It is cooler than in the city. Egrets (some with the orange stripe of mating season), black storks, and ibises lift off the floor of the savanna near a watercourse, the iconic symbol of the sub-Saharan plain.

There the roads are virtually empty of motorized vehicles, but full of children and women walking with their burdens, and men walking to stands selling tea. Now and then the occasional open-bed truck, full of men going to labor somewhere, passes. The men barely notice the visitors on the road.

But the West is also home to three major cities. Al Fasher, capital of North Darfur, with its pizza parlor and shops selling bottled water, has a population (in 2006, according to Thomas Brinkhoff's City Population web site) of about 265,000. Once a caravan center, Al Fasher dates from the 18th century when a sultan's palace attracted settlers. El Geneina, capital of West Darfur, is 15 miles from the Chad border. Its population has swollen in recent years to some 163,000 with the influx of displaced peoples from other regions of Sudan. Kiosks sell soap, sugar, batteries, and cigarettes. Its airport connects travelers to other regional cities and Khartoum. Nyala, with its markets, mosques, and humanitarian offices is home to about 227,000 people, and is the capital city of South Darfur. Nyala also has an airport, with daily humanitarian flights and a few commercial flights each week.

In Southern Sudan, Juba is the major city, and the historic capital of that region. Estimates of its population range from 163,000 to 250,000. West of Juba, Rumbek is the administrative capital of the Southern Sudan government. Pinpointing population levels in Sudan is difficult due in part to the numbers of displaced persons as well as to the lack of a formal census until April 2008.

Across the midsection of Sudan lies the transitional zone of the Sahel, stretching from the Atlantic borders of Senegal and Mauritania to the Red Sea, from Dakar to Port Sudan. Sahel is an Arabic word that means "shore." The Sahel marks a broad border between the arid red-gold sands of the Sahara and Nubian deserts to the North and the tropical climes and humid forests of the South. Sudan's topography ranges from the ever-wet swamps of the Sudd in the South to several ranges of bald, rocky mountains in North Darfur and Southern Sudan. Much of Sudan is flat savanna, home to many wild birds and animals.

The Challenge of Making a Portrait of Sudan

The paradoxes of Sudan challenge any Western writer, and any Western reader, in several ways. That each of these challenges could fill its own book is a measure of their complexity. The Bibliography suggests resources for readers who want to go deeper.

For one, the situation in all of Sudan in 2008, when this study was written, was very fluid. A fragile peace was on the breaking point, and a peace accord for Darfur had neither been signed by all nor was being observed by many of the actors in that region. Humanitarian efforts seemed to be under siege by the insecurity, the uncertainties of war, and the ongoing violence. A rebellion was brewing in the South Kordofan, spurred by discontent among marginalized Nuba people. Two key elections were approaching that could change the course of Sudan: general elections in 2009 and a referendum on the autonomy of Southern Sudan in 2011. Whatever is written about events in 2008 may be completely out of date when the Schools of Christian Mission convene in 2009 to study Sudan.

- A second challenge is that Western values are not shared by the majority of people living in Sudan. As an example, Sudanese women, and other African women define their roles and what they need and find appropriate for their empowerment differently from many Western women. Many African women see their leadership as organically connected to their nurture and support of family life. This contention comes from an African scholar, Mary E. Modupe Kolawole. "There is still a lot that the West needs to know about Africa," she wrote—especially to dispel "distorted images and misrepresentations of African women." Misunderstandings can arise because of these differences in approach.

- For another, racial and religious prejudice may distort Western understandings of Africa in general, and of Sudan in particular. As an example, the people of Sudan are nearly all Muslim, with smaller populations of people who practice traditional African religions. Southern Sudan is predominately Christian. Many Sudanese engage in polygyny, the practice of marriage to more than one woman at a time. There are misconceptions about Islam itself—suspicions that as a religion it oppresses women, for instance. Though it is culture that is the true culprit here, many Westerners simply do not distinguish among the nuances. Islam has also received less-than-flattering media coverage in recent years, especially its association in media reports with the war on terrorism. How these latter images have played out in the national consciousness of Westerners was neatly summed up in former President George W. Bush's triune "axis of evil." We can recall that this "axis" included two predominantly Muslim countries.

Women use a large mortar and pestle to pound okra into powder that will be used to thicken soup or sauces.

(Paul Jeffrey, UMCOR)

> Sudan is virtually two countries in one, governed under the banners of the government of national unity from Khartoum; and the government of Southern Sudan, administered since a 2005 peace agreement at Rumbek and Juba.
>
> All these places and peoples, city and outlands, Sahel and tropics, North and South, ethnic groups and foreign workers, create the diverse fabric of Sudan.

- Politics such as the above affect how we relate to the news and the values of another culture, and that presents a fourth challenge. Virtually every piece of information about Sudan comes from organizations that have a political or cultural agenda. Very little commentary is free from the coloration of a particular political viewpoint. Complicating this fact is that these are viewpoints from people who are making efforts to do what is right. Even what we name a movement or a people can suggest an agenda. An example is, what to call the people fighting in Darfur. Rebels? Insurgents? Freedom fighters? All have connotations for good or ill. No term, no concept, in Sudan can be divorced from its political and social implications. So bringing an attentiveness or even healthy skepticism to one's reading on Sudan is advisable.

The need for such thoughtful questions has been especially obvious in the coverage of the position of advocacy groups like Save Darfur and Enough (both of which advocate for prosecution and isolation of the Sudanese government) and the conflict they have created for relief agencies working on the ground in Sudan. A *Los Angeles Times* essay, circulated widely in mid-2007, pointed out that an advertising campaign of the activist group

Save Darfur could be endangering humanitarian workers on the ground by calling for a "no-fly" zone over Sudan. In the opinion of the essayist, the enactment of such a no-fly zone could jeopardize the provision of vital humanitarian assistance to millions. Similar tensions between human rights groups and humanitarian groups existed during other conflicts—Kosovo, for example, and Afghanistan.

It is important to remember that neutrality is central to humanitarian work. Even the word "intervention" raises questions about neutrality because it suggests a confrontation, rather than an offer of relief. Human rights activism and humanitarian aid may be incompatible in this sense, and this is a challenge for people of faith who may see their duty in both arenas.

- Another issue to be grappled with is the use of the term genocide. Like other confrontational labels, that word is not compatible with the offering of humanitarian relief and aid. United Methodist Committee on Relief, the denomination's aid agency, does not use the word in connection with Sudan because of the danger it poses to aid workers in Darfur and Southern Sudan. Also contesting the use of the term are other aid agencies as well as the UN. The term is explored in this study with that caveat.

- Finally, stereotypes of Africa affect Western thinking. Think back to your first images of Africa: those portrayals of "The Dark Continent"; those outworn ideas about native people whose innate dignity and cultural heritage were quashed with mistreatment, slavery and worse; false images of people unable to think creatively about peace—chaotic and incompetent. Westerners may be tempted to make judgments about Sudanese people based on these stereotypes and misconceptions or even suspicions about them.

The goal of this mission study is to invite you to appreciate the complexities and to be in solidarity with all the people of Sudan as you befriend the United Methodist churches there and celebrate their courage. And it is a call to pray for the realization of a nation's dream of peace. Chapter One will introduce readers to the complex tapestry of Sudan's history, natural resources, and offer some clues about the roots of conflict there. Chapter Two highlights the major tribes of North and South and their livelihoods, customs, and vulnerabilities, while also exploring stories of individuals caught and displaced by the conflicts. Since many Sudanese are devout Muslims, a brief primer on Islam further sets a context for readers. Using a variety of viewpoints and sources, Chapter Three examines the politics of war and peace in Sudan, summarizing the key issues and myths of the recent wars. Chapter Four details some entry points for persons and groups interested in fostering the dream of peace. Chapter Five asks how the church, both in Sudan and in the United States, can use its moral authority to create a culture of peace in Sudan.

Theologian Sally McFague encouraged people of faith to view differences with others with a "loving eye" rather than the "arrogant eye" sometimes brought to discourse about differences. So we proceed with the recognition that the challenges to our understanding are greater and more complex than can be fully addressed in this study. With humility, and with hope that readers will bring their loving eye, we invite you to explore something of Sudan, a place so ancient yet so full of modern contradictions, to learn the why, where, how, who, and what of the core issues that embody and inspirit many of the issues of the 21st century continent of Africa— and why the beauty and courage of its people promise the hope that eventually the dream of peace will be realized there.

Water is a precious resource in Sudan, often collected at great hazard to women and children who may have to walk up to 17 kilometers to obtain their daily needs.
(Paul Jeffrey, UMCOR)

Chapter One
A Sense of Place

Setting the Stage

The country we call Sudan is the home of an ancient civilization. In the Hebrew Testament the land bordering the Red Sea below Egypt was known as the land of Kush. In fact, Numbers 12:1 suggests that a wife of Moses (the text does not name her) was a Kushite woman. The center of Kush culture was at Merowe, about 100 miles north of the confluence of the Blue and White Niles. Khartoum, Sudan's capital city, lies at the confluence now. Sudan is the largest country in Africa, known as the Republic of Sudan or, in Arabic, the lingua franca of Sudan, Jumhuriyat as-Sudan. The short form, Sudan, is most often used in the West. The short form in Sudan is as-Sudan.

Human populations have lived there for at least nine million years. Some historians believe Sudan, not the Euphrates area, may have been the "cradle of civilization." Homer, the Greek poet, knew of the region, and Greek merchants visited there to trade their cloth and wines for gum arabic, spices, and slaves. The Roman emperor Nero ordered troops to reconnoiter far up the Nile but when they encountered the Sudd, or swamp, in what is now Southern Sudan, they gave up plans to conquer the region. During the 7th century reign of Justinian, another Roman emperor, many Sudanese kingdoms were converted to Christianity. It is said that churches followed the long path of the Nile until Islam reached this area in the 16th century.

Almost from its very beginnings the place has been the center of tribal, ethnic, and international struggles for dominance and control of resources and land. In its 5,000 year history the region we know today as Sudan has been at peace for only about 600 years.

Riches and Resources

As a whole, Sudan is rich in natural resources, such as oil and rich farmland. The hospitable, near-tropical climate in Southern Sudan could supply food for the entire country. Many people work on large mechanized farms, irrigated and controlled by the government of Sudan. But the backbone of the rural economy is the small farm, often cultivated by hand and dependent on favorable rains. Agriculture employs nearly 80 percent of the workforce. With persistent drought, especially in the regions north of the Sahel, water is a critical resource for people, their animals, and their crops. When Boston University researchers in July 2007 disclosed the discovery of an underground lake the size of Lake Erie in North Darfur, the question of whether such water wealth had the potential to harm the region or help it was an authentic concern.

Still, Sudan's economy is booming with increased production and export of oil. An oil pipeline runs nearly 1,000 miles from the oilfields in Southern Sudan's Al Wahdah (Unity) State to Port Sudan on the Red Sea. A second pipeline, from Southern Sudan's Upper Nile State, merges with the long line near Khartoum. Small reserves of uranium, iron ore, copper, chromium, zinc, tungsten, mica, silver, and gold are among other natural resources. Sudan also exports livestock, cotton, sesame, groundnuts, gum arabic, and sugar to markets such as China, Saudi Arabia, the United Arab Emirates, Germany, India, and France.

Sociological Contrasts

Sociologically and ethnically, Sudan's 40 million inhabitants themselves are a study in contrast. Though most are Muslim, they are Muslims of many persuasions. Most are Sunni Muslim. Some adhere to the ancient Sufi tradition of Islam. Those who practice Sufism accept different cultural practices and behaviors of others.

Some Muslims adhere to fundamentalist interpretations of Islam and cultures that impose strong punishments for seemingly mild infractions. Yet others practice a moderate Islam. About a quarter of Sudanese people practice traditional religions such as animism. And some are Christian—the exact number is in dispute—the result of 19th and 20th century missionary activity in Southern Sudan. Some Sudanese to this day combine Christian observances with the traditional observances and practices of their pre-missionary beliefs, especially in family life, song, dance, and feasts.

Second-Class Citizens?

Peace in Sudan has proved elusive. Colonization by ancient Egyptians in the time of the Pharaohs, Turko-Egyptians, and then by the British in joint dominion with Egypt, continued the stamp of instability and simmering resentments upon Sudan, that had begun with conquest in Sudan's early history. The region was considered a sort of backwater. During colonial times in the 19th century the "Arabized" Sudanese were not viewed by Arabs from the Middle East or Egypt as "true" Arabs but were—and continue to be—accorded a sort of second-class status. Loyalty to the colonial governors was difficult to command among the many tribes and factions, adding to this perception. The Southerners of Sudan, where the missionaries had operated, were perceived even more poorly than Northerners. Slave traders from the Mediterranean region as well as from the North raided Southern settlements. Racist policies of the ruling government fomented war, as did severe limits on Southerners' voice in government and sharing of resources.

The Nile River, born in the convergence of the Blue Nile and the White Nile in Khartoum city, became a lodestone for wealth and power. Along the Nile, and in the city overlooking the merger of these two important watercourses, the wealthy riverine tribes congregated. Their lifestyle, forged in important suburbs like Omdurman where a new *souk*, or market, offers the riches of the globe, is the polar opposite to the extremes of poverty of farm people and pastoralists in rural Sudan.

Town and Country: Regions, Towns, and Infrastructure

In 2008 Sudan had 25 administrative divisions or states. They are usually named in a Latinized Arabic. This may change if Southern Sudan chooses self-determination in 2011, one of the options of the Comprehensive Peace Agreement.

Like many countries in Africa with similar circumstances, Sudan is a country of the young. The median age is under 20 years, and life expectancy for the total population is estimated at just over 50 years of age. Contributing to the relatively short life expectancy are war, poverty, hunger, and lack of access to medical care.

There are about 1,000 miles of railroad track in the North, and virtually no rail transport in the South. Most of the railways serve as conduits for transporting the harvests of cotton plantations. Much of the track, like the few paved roadways, has been damaged in the years of war, due to lack of maintenance. Also the track is old—installed between 1890 and 1920 during British-Egyptian colonial times.

A Short History

Sudan is a culture of oral history. Families, especially in rural areas, can recall their histories for many generations in the past. We know that around 3000 BCE ["Before the Common Era," or, in traditional terms, "Before Christ" (BC)], the area called Nubia by the Greeks, and Kush by the Egyptians and Israelites, was controlled by the ruling Pharaohs. Then, as Egypt declined during

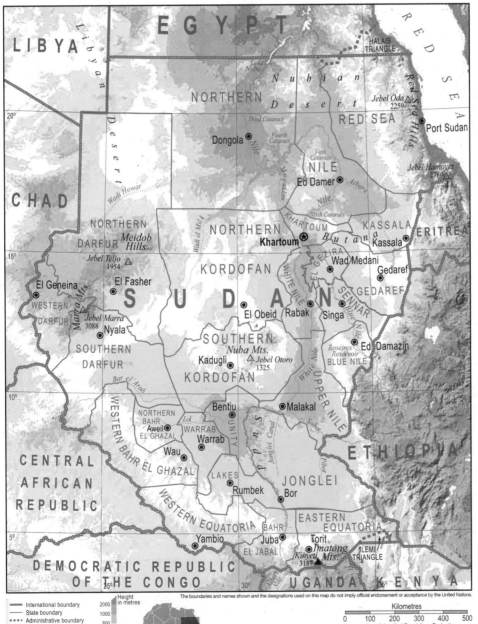

Sudan is the largest country in Africa, comparable to the eastern half of the US.

Photo: Sudan, no. 3707, Rev. 10 April 2007. United Nations Cartographic Section, http://www.un.org/Depts/ Cartographic/french/htmain.htm

the 8th century BCE, rulers of the country to the south conquered Egypt. Their rule lasted about 200 years, and from the disintegration of that country, three autonomous states prefiguring modern-day Sudan arose: Nobatia, Dongola, and Alodia. The economies of these predominantly Christian, culturally independent, states were based on trade of goods from equatorial Africa to the Mediterranean and Europe. Invading Arabs introduced Muslim preaching and a treaty with Dongola that lasted 600 years. But in the 14th century CE [the "Common Era," or, more traditionally, "Anno Domini" (AD)], Egyptian Mamelukes conquered Dongola and Alodia, and new Islamic territories came into being. Darfur, far to the west on the edge of the Sahara desert, was one of them.

Egypt, backed by Britain, fought for control of the entire country, and by 1876 the country was united under the name Sudan, a word with its origins in the Arabic *a'soud*, meaning literally "country of Blacks." Coherent, culturally rich societies became fragmented as smaller local governments and established religious communities were forced to cede much of their power to the new conquerors. Britain, through co-opting its colonies' armies and the minds and hearts of community leaders, intended to bring much of Africa—from Cairo to Cape Town—within its rule. The scramble for Africa was on, as parallel events in many other kingdoms and regions of the African continent occurred during the latter third of the 19th century, most for the purpose of exploiting resources.

An armed uprising led by Muhammad Ahmad—known to most people as the "Mahdi" after the Qur'an prophecy of a redeemer of Islam—in 1881 defeated British troops in Khartoum in a drive to restore Islamic rule. The Ahmad government prevailed for 13 years, but fell in attacks by Egyptian and British armies. To

Residents of the Hamidiya displaced persons camp near Zalingei, in Sudan's war-torn Darfur region, crowd round a water distribution system installed by ACT-Caritas.
(Paul Jeffrey, ACT-Caritas)

consolidate their power, the British effectively divided Sudan's North from South.

When independence from British-Egyptian rule was achieved in 1956, the southern provinces, with claims of political and economic marginalization, declared war against the new government. Tens of thousands were killed or displaced over the 16 years of conflict. Brokering the 1972 peace talks at Addis Ababa were officials of the World Council of Churches and the All Africa Conference of Churches.

That period of peace was short. Though accords granting more autonomy to the South ended the war for a time, the government did not follow through with its promises. A declaration of Islamic law (sharia) by the centralized government in Khartoum recharged the Southern guerrilla movement, kindling anew the quest for political autonomy and religious freedom for all ethnic groups and regions both North and South in a "New Sudan." Twenty more years of exceptionally cruel war—fought in Southern Sudan largely off camera and outside the attention span of most Westerners—caused the death of nearly two million people, and displaced three million. The displaced fled in all directions—toward Uganda, the Central African Republic, Kenya, Egypt, and Ethiopia; internally toward Darfur and north to Khartoum; and some to Australia, Canada, and the United States.

Withholding power, religious freedoms, and economic advantages from the South by the Northern government continued through two coups. The current president of Sudan, Omar Hassan al-Bashir, attained power in 1989 through one of the coups, dissolving political parties and violently dispatching opponents. Since 1989, as for so many years before, Sudan's people have suffered from the cruelties of war in one way or another.

Sudan Fast Facts
(Adapted from the *CIA Factbook*, May 2008)

Land Area: North and South, roughly the area of the United States east of the Mississippi River

Population: North and South, 40,218,455 people (July 2008 estimate). Darfur approximately 7,400,000 people

Median Age: 18.9 years

Life Expectancy: 50 years

Women over the age of 65: 471,530

Men over the age of 65: 518,822

Cellular phones in use: 4.7 million
(2006 estimate)

Main occupations: Agriculture (80 percent)
Industry (7 percent)
Services (13 percent)

Religions: Muslim, 70 percent
Christian, 5 percent
Traditional beliefs, 25 percent

Languages: Arabic (official)
more than 540 others, including Nubian, Ta Bedawie, diverse Nilotic, Nilo-Hamitic, and Sudanic dialects, English

Number of women over age 15 who can read and write: 5,932,344 (2003 estimate)

Girls skip rope in front of their school in the Dereig Camp for internally displaced persons.
(Paul Jeffrey, ACT-Caritas)

According to Gerard Prunier, the renowned Horn of Africa analyst who founded a center for African Studies at the University of Addis Ababa, as Omar al-Bashir took power, he began reaching out to other Arab leaders in the Mediterranean region, such as Muammar al Gaddafi, the president of Libya. Gaddafi wanted control of Darfur as a base for an incursion into Chad. President al-Bashir wanted to further his interest in consolidation of Islamist control. The two signed a treaty that on paper ceded Darfur to Libya.

But not long after the events of 9/11 happened, Prunier believes that Omar al-Bashir understood that a US president who was set to invade Afghanistan to punish perpetrators of the 9/11 attacks might welcome his assistance with the only thing he had to offer—information. He had already seen to the departure of Osama bin Ladin, who had lived in Khartoum from 1990 until 1996. Under the Clinton administration, the US had bombed a pharmaceutical factory in Khartoum. President al-Bashir may have worried that the US would again target his country. So, ironically, Sudan for a time became a valuable ally of the West, a departure from its previous prominent place on a list of states that sponsor terrorism. Omar al-Bashir followed a strategy of providing intelligence to the US about people suspected of terrorism and assisting the United States in achieving its objectives in the fight against terrorism.

In this context the peace negotiations to end the long Southern war began in Nairobi in 2002. Negotiations were facilitated by the Intergovernmental Authority on Development peace process, a regional initiative based on a declaration of principles that provided the framework for the agreement. Kenya chaired the IGAD process, joined by mediators from Eritrea, Ethiopia, and Uganda. Norway and the United Kingdom played key roles. US involvement was necessary to insure a settlement.

Peace at Last?

The peace agreement signed in January 2005 by the government of Sudan and the Southern Peoples' Liberation Army granted Southern Sudan autonomy for six years, and an equal share of oil. The agreement did not include Darfur, where a rebellion against the government had been fought for several years—military activity relatively unnoticed since 2002. Humanitarian and government observers hoped the agreement for

Southern Sudan would positively affect the situation in Darfur as well.

In March 2005 United Methodist Committee on Relief joined other international aid organizations providing humanitarian assistance, with operations in Darfur and an office in Khartoum. The peace agreement had created a co-vice presidency, which was to be filled by John Garang. Three weeks after being sworn in, Garang was killed in a helicopter crash. There were riots in Khartoum. But the peace held. However, in Darfur, the International Crisis Group reported that disorganization and lack of leadership among the splinter groups made it easy for the government to manipulate traditional tribal leaders in its search for ways to weaken the rebellion. The Crisis Group report contended that successive Sudanese governments have used localized conflicts to perpetuate the hegemony of the northern elites, in order to keep Darfur and other peripheral regions marginalized. The International Crisis Group, founded in 1995 to monitor the crisis in Bosnia, is an independent, nonpartisan source of analysis and advice to governments and intergovernmental bodies like the United Nations, the European Union and the World Bank, on prevention or resolution of conflicts. The ICG has actively reported on Sudan, particularly Darfur, and has recommended reforms of the peace process.

The Insurgency in Darfur

As the war resurfaced in Darfur, it began attracting attention from Western media in late 2003. The harsh response of the government of Sudan to quell what it saw as an insurgency appalled international observers. New stories of aircraft bombing villages, raids by mounted militias (sometimes called *janjaweed*), looting, and violence against persons, created a more or less permanent war in Sudan. In 2006 the Sudanese government and one wing of Darfur's largest rebel groups, the Sudan Liberation Movement, signed a Darfur peace agreement. One of the principal leaders of the Sudan Liberation Movement, Minni Arkoi Minnawi, became President al-Bashir's advisor on Darfur. Minnawi's life has been threatened by the other leaders who did not sign off on the agreement. They object that he now takes the part of the government on their issues.

Competing rebel groups continued to hold out, so that as of 2008 the peace agreement for Darfur remained unsigned by all but one. The ongoing splintering of these competing factions may be a deliberate strategy benefiting one or more of the parties while keeping up the appearance of peacemaking. In 2008 there were mixed reports on the number of groups, but the commander of peacekeeping troops estimated there were about 30 active groups, "with no cohesive command or control." In the meantime, the violence continued, though at a somewhat reduced rate. The UN Special Rapporteur on the human rights situation in Sudan, Sima Samar, issued a report in July 2008 that recounted violence in both Southern Sudan and in Darfur. "I strongly condemn the reported use of child soldiers" in these attacks, she wrote. "The use of children under 15 as combatants constitutes a serious violation of international law." For her report Ms. Samar visited Darfur. She identified positive steps taken by the government, such as increasing the number of women police and increased activities of the State Committees against sexual and gender violence. "Despite such positive steps, the human rights situation on the ground remains grim. Direct violations by government forces continue to be reported.... There is no military solution to the Darfur conflict," she wrote. An attack in Darfur while Ms. Samar was there caused her to cite the inability of the peacekeepers—with their inadequate numbers and resources—to intervene in violence against civilians. In Chapter Three we will examine Darfur in more detail.

Chapter Two
The People

The Cultural Tapestry of Sudan

The Lion, Hyena, and Fox were friends. When they went out hunting together, they killed a donkey, an ariel, and a hare. The Lion said to the Hyena, "How shall we divide the kill among us?" The Hyena said, "I know all about dividing a kill. You take the donkey, I will take the ariel, and Fox can have the hare." The Lion was angry and struck the Hyena so hard that she died. Then he called the Fox and said to her, "Divide the kill." The Fox said, "The donkey will do for your lunch, and the ariel for your dinner, and you can wipe your mouth with the hare." The Lion was very pleased and said, "O Fox, who taught you this division?" The Fox replied, "The fate of the Hyena taught me."—*Nuer Folk Tale*

This folk tale from the Nuer illustrates the wisdom and humor of the people of Sudan, part of the country's rich tapestry of cultures, ethnicities, and traditions. The Nuer are one of the larger confederations of tribes in Southern Sudan.

Major Tribes of the South

The Nuer live in clusters of communities along the banks of the Nile River. Primarily cattle farmers, they supplement their diets with millet and fish. They split their time between riverside settlements in dry seasons, and higher-ground villages in flood seasons. Linguists describe the Nuer language as "Eastern Sudanic," and associate the Nuer with other Nilo-Saharan tribal families. Traditional Nuer families are polygynous. Religious worship among Nuers who did not convert to Christianity honors a single creator thought to be all-surrounding but also to take form in some plants and animals.

Like the Nuer, the Dinka people—at 4 million the largest tribal grouping in Southern Sudan and one of the most ancient—count their wealth in cattle. As pastoral people the Dinka, called *Jieng* in their own language, migrate regularly as do their Nuer neighbors, cultivating crops during the rainy season in villages built on high ground, and sheltering and feeding their cattle in the riverine pasture land in dry season. Traditional buildings in the more permanent settlements above the Nile's floodplain are mud-walled, topped with a conical thatch of reeds and grasses. Dinka children learn the history of their people through folk tales, poetry, and songs. Non-Christian and non-Muslim Dinka worship the life-giving god, Nhial, whom they can contact through intermediaries in rituals conducted by tribal members who have the gifts of healing and divination. Ancestors are also believed to be sources of strength in everyday life.

The Misseriya, traditionally known as Arab, are the neighbors of the Dinka and Nuer. They were among the migrants into Sudan from the East in the 18th century and brought to the region the practice of moving their cattle between pasturelands in the South and the North in response to seasonal changes. Tensions between the Dinka and Misseriya over grazing rights, power sharing, and other political and economic considerations are not new. A 2007 agreement signed in Abyei, South Kordofan, by Misseriya and Dinka traders to form one chamber of commerce was a celebrated breakthrough in peacebuilding. According to Human Rights Watch, though, continued fighting months after the accord resulted in Abyei's being burned to the ground in May 2008.

Altogether the Shilluk and their White Nile neighbors, the Nuer and the Dinka, make up about 20 percent of

Sudan's total population. Related by language to the others, the Shilluk hunt, herd cattle and goats, and grow staple grains such as millet in their settlements along the west banks of the Nile. Like the Nuer, the Shilluk are monotheistic, with the belief that the creative force is symbolized in real life by certain animals, plants, and signs.

Major Tribes of the North

There are Arab and non-Arab groups in the North—but as an article on Sudan in the *Encyclopedia Britannica* points out, "ethnic identity may not actually coincide with a particular racial character." In other words, most Sudanese who self-identify as Arabs are a mix of ethnicities. They share a common language and religion but little else. They live in diverse circumstances, from urban to rural. The wealthy riverine groups—for example, the Jaali, Beja, and Misseriya—are the elite who control the Khartoum government. If any group in the North could be called indigenous, it is the Fur. The powerful kingdoms of the Fur in the 1500s extended to the Nile, 700 miles to the east. The Fur controlled the trading and economic center for the mountainous western regions known as Jebbal Marra. Late in the 16th century an Islamic sultanate took over, and the Fur adopted Arabic language, religious practices, and dress. Today they are entirely Muslim, though are considered "non-Arab," because even with intermarriage with other ethnicities their heritage is that of indigenous people of the region. Land is the marker of wealth, and the very wealthy few practice polygyny.

The Nuba people—a non-Arab group of more than 60 different tribes totaling some million and a half—farm crops like millet, sorghum, sesame, and groundnuts on terraces and basins in the broad central region lying between Darfur in the West and the White Nile River valley in the East. The Nuba also raise cattle, sheep, and goats. In the southern core of Nuba territory, kinship is determined through women; northward, this shifts to identity through the male line. Nuba people are a mixture of Christian, Muslim, and traditional African religions. The sharp, steep granite hills of the Nuba Mountains serve as a topographical border between South and North.

A rebellion by the Nuba could become the next Darfur. In the early 1990s the Nuba were pushed out of their traditional homelands into so-called "peace villages" in South Kordofan. These villages are government camps or holding areas for Nuba laborers working at the huge mechanized farms in that region. The Nuba are in effect working their own land to enrich not their families, but the wealth of investors in the government of Sudan. Such appropriation of lands by outsiders is an old story in Sudan, stemming from colonial occupation by the British and Egyptians. The postcolonial governments of Sudan since 1956 have continued these practices. Lydia Polgreen, a journalist who has written about the Sahel and sub-Saharan Africa for many years, wrote in *The New York Times* that successors to Great Britain "had the blessing of the World Bank and the International Monetary Fund" to seize "vast tracts of land in the name of agricultural development, turning farmers who worked their own land into wage laborers." No wonder the Nuba nurse grievances that could boil over!

Confirming Polgreen's observation is Hafiz Mohammed, who is Sudan coordinator for Justice Africa, a research institute run by, for, and with Africans. In an article for Africa Files, a network of advocates for social justice in the African continent, Mohammed wrote in 2008 that "most Nuba were not happy about what they got out of the peace agreement....Some of them considered [it] a sell-out." He pointed out that oil revenues were to fund development. But "there is no sign of development."

Another non-Arab Muslim group is the Zaghawa tribe. The Zaghawa live north of the Fur in the border areas of Sudan and Chad. Living as neighbors there is an Arab group, the *Baqqarah* (an Arabic word meaning "cattle herders") who are descendents of Egyptian Arabs. The *Baqqarah* (also spelled *Baggarah*) probably migrated into Darfur and other northern regions during the 18th century.

What Does It Mean to Be Arab in Sudan?

Western journalists have made much of the meanings of Arab and non-Arab or African in reporting on the ongoing strife in Sudan, especially in attempting to analyze causes for the violence. The assumption that a common language and religion could be a mobilizing factor for people calling themselves Arab led to some questionable assignments of motive, cause, and effect; for example, early stories about the war in Darfur stemming from religious conflicts. Nearly all people in Sudan are ethnically mixed. Intermarriage among neighboring groups ensured this diverse mix. Many Northern people who describe themselves as Arab are physically indistinguishable from people in the South and elsewhere who are non-Arab. All are dark-skinned and dark-haired and share similar facial features of other peoples in Africa.

In a post-9/11 world Arab origins can stir righteous anger and moral indignation. The conflicts of Sudan, especially the war in Darfur, seem to engender an angry and indignant response from observers and activists in the US. Ironically the focus on a "distant, weak, and safely nonwhite target" recalls the righteous anger directed against Arab slave traders operating in Africa in the 19th century as European countries prepared to grab what they could of Africa's land, labor, and raw materials. Back then Europe's indignation over Arab slave

The Ethnicities and Cultures of Sudan

For more detail on customs, languages, and community life, see *Encyclopædia Britannica Online* listings for specific population groups, and the long article entitled "The Sudan," from which the descriptions in the sections "Major Tribes of the South" and "Major Tribes of the North" were drawn. Refer to the Bibliography for full citations.

trading masked its growing desire for African colonies. Today, as we will see in Chapter Three, indignation about Sudanese Arab involvement in the 21st century's unresolved conflicts of Darfur may mask a desire for access to Sudanese resources.

Women carry water home from a well in Geles, an Arab village in Darfur where an ecumenical coalition has provided wells and a variety of other services.
(Paul Jeffrey, ACT-Caritas)

Listen to the Voices of Africans

One way to enlarge our understanding of people whose cultures and life experiences are very different from our own is to listen. In this section is an opportunity to listen to the voices and stories of Africans as told by several Sudanese women and men interviewed in 2005. Some were displaced and living in camps. One was living in a small house in Khartoum, able to find skilled work because of a good education.

Saba Recalls Life "Before"

In quiet Arabic Saba recounted her story of life before the war for guests at the Khartoum office of the United Methodist Committee on Relief. By "before," she meant before men on horseback plundered rural Zalingei in West Darfur, Sudan. Some of Saba's family fled eastward on foot, and by lorry, when they were lucky.

One of Millions Displaced

For Saba the gunmen put a face on the war that over decades has displaced millions like her. At the United Nations some say from two million to four million, the largest number of internally displaced people in the world.

Making the near-thousand-mile trek to Khartoum were Saba and her three sons, ages two to seven, and her two brothers. They faced dangers of banditry and mechanical breakdowns on the road. In 2005 they lived in Mayo, one of six camps for displaced persons in the capital, part of the 250,000 or so displaced persons living in Khartoum camps. The camps were off limits to visitors to the capital region. Saba hunted for work by going door-to-door. She earned a few dinars a day when she could clean someone's house or labor as a laundry worker.

A member of her extended family introduced Saba to UMCOR. Since February 2005 UMCOR's new office in Sudan has implemented agriculture programs in South Darfur, helping people like Saba's parents to regain their self-sufficiency. As part of its normal practice UMCOR staffs its headquarters in Khartoum and its field operations in South Darfur and Yei, in Southern Sudan, with local workers.

Home Still Calls

Saba recalled a vastly different life on the family land. Before the war her father was a traditional farmer in Zalingei. He raised goats and cows not for the market but to meet family needs. When Saba left, four sisters stayed behind to care for the parents. She had no way to contact them, but she knew that little remained of their old life. The animals were stolen or run off by the gunmen, wells were polluted, houses burned, people killed. Still, Saba's wish—like 54 percent of her compatriots—is to return home.

Life Issues: Health, Food, Water, Sustainability

A Northern Story: Julha Farm

A light rain stirred the fronds of millet and the serrated leaves of groundnut plants that cover the red sand of Julha, a women's farm in Ed Daein, South Darfur.

About a dozen women cultivated their ground on an August morning in 2005. Some of them bent to the hoe with a child wrapped artfully on their backs in a tight sling. Earlier in the day they had already brought water to the camp in jerry cans supplied by United Methodist Committee on Relief. Their seed came from UMCOR, too. The hoes they were using were hammered out on an open fire by local blacksmiths near El Ferdous, a community of displaced Darfurians and their hosts. Near the end of the day, the women carried firewood in bundles of 20 to 30 sticks, bound with cords of reeds, perfectly balanced on their heads. Just another day at Julha, which means forehead.

Women's Self-Sufficiency: Good for Recovery

Teaching women to be self-sufficient is a first step in a community's turnaround after decades of instability, said Jane Ohuma, UMCOR's head of mission in Sudan. Women can influence the nutrition of entire families, for instance. When they gain confidence from learning new farming skills, they transmit that confidence, the skills, and even extra income to their families. In a culture where the life of a woman is undervalued, self-sufficiency leads to important strides forward.

Each head of household at Julha received two measures, or in the local terminology *malwas*, of millet to plant in the sandy soil and one *malwa* of sorghum to plant in clay—altogether enough for about four hectares. Teaching them to intercrop, or mingle, these plantings with other seeds, such as groundnuts and beans, was the UMCOR agronomist, Abdul Rahim Malik. Okra and melon seeds are interplanted as cash crops. The half dozen families at Julha, all headed by women, are growing all of these. The rains have been good, harbinger of a bumper crop.

"We Would Like to See Those We Left"

Farms like Julha dot the savanna of this part of South Darfur where UMCOR started the seeds and tools program with a grant from a remarkable congregation, the Ginghamsburg United Methodist Church in Ohio. (In August 2005 some 5,200 families had crops under cultivation. The number today has reached over 10,000.) Many, like the women at Julha, lived at the farm sites, since the plots are too far from the camp at El Ferdous to walk back and forth. A few *gotia*, the conical brush structures that serve as shelters, are scattered around the edge of the field.

Angelina put down her hoe and adjusted her son to her other shoulder. She pronounced her name with a hard "g," a remnant of colonial schooling in her home state of Bahr al Ghazal, south of where she stood now at Julha. Her story, told so unflinchingly, was like many others: murdered relatives, sacked village, fleeing in fear. And like other displaced persons in South Darfur, Angelina longed to go home.

What was at home that she didn't have at Julha? "The people we left behind," she said. "We left when we were very young. We would like to see those we left."

Sleeping in Shifts

Musayahia's sculpted cheekbones topped a small beard and moustache. He dressed in the style of many Khartoum men, a loose shirt and trousers, and a pair of loafer-like *markoub*, traditional goat-leather shoes.

He had enjoyed a good education. In 2005 he was in a Khartoum school studying science, math, Arabic, English, geography, and history. He was lucky to have found a place to live in Mamora, a section of Khartoum away from the camps. He built a *rakouba* made of pickets and a small dwelling for his wife, son, and father. He sent money to his mother and a sister still living in Darfur.

En route from Darfur two years earlier, after militias attacked his village, he traveled with seventeen others. It was rainy season, and the road was often washed out. They watched over one another, sleeping in shifts in the open so someone was always awake to alert the others to suspicious sounds. They camped at night, traveling only during daylight hours. It took 15 days to traverse the 700 miles by lorry.

"I am in school now to improve my life, to find a suitable job," Musayahia said. "It's expensive to live in Khartoum, but safer. I hope that the peace agreement (signed a few months before) will mean peace for Darfur as well." Though he lost his house and had to separate his family, he too wanted to return home.

Tribes and Social Connections

Sudan is a land of diverse languages, tribal relationships, and social arrangements. The Joshua Project, a web-based data site sponsored by the US Center for World Mission, estimates there are at least 244 distinct ethnic groups, speaking 169 languages. Some place the count even higher—up to 583 tribal peoples, speaking some 400 different languages or dialects. In Southern Sudan, virtually a separate country, the five major ethnic groups speak at least 100 languages.

Governance in the regions far from the Northern capital, Khartoum, relies on historic tribal and social connections more than official mandates. In Darfur, for example, a number of powerful leaders, called sultans, oversee regional *omdas*—leaders who are responsible for several villages in an area. Individual village headmen are known as sheikhs. Social interaction, sharing of resources, and even intermarriage among various tribal members, are commonplace. Disputes traditionally are settled by the respected sultans, *omdas*, and sheikhs. These customs can be traced to the 1500s when the sultanates of Darfur extended well into what is now known as Chad.

In Southern Sudan villages are led by elders, or judges, elected not by formal ballot but through a community consensus of respect and appreciation for their integrity and sense of fairness. Judges typically determine the outcome of land ownership disputes, grazing rights, and clashes over water use. Christian missionaries, both Roman Catholic and Anglican, began working in Southern Sudan in the 1800s. By the time in 1983 that the national government declared all of Sudan would live under sharia law, Christians constituted a majority of inhabitants in Southern Sudan, though only a small minority in the whole of the country.

Some Sudan analysts today maintain that the Northern government uses a strategy of deliberate destabilization to disrupt these traditional forms of social organization. For example Daoud Hari, memoir writer and translator for many Western journalists trying to report on the unfolding humanitarian crisis in Darfur, predicts that "when the government [of Sudan] has removed or killed all the traditional non-Arabs, then it will get the traditional Arabs to fight one another so they too will disappear from valuable lands." Hari maintains this is the way most people in his extended family and associates see it, and his analysis helps to dispel the notion that conflict in Sudan has to do with Arab and non-Arab categories seized on by Western journalists early on. Hari means that the government is interested in retaining whatever resources there are for itself.

Perhaps it is not a coincidence that more than 40 competing militia, at work from Darfur through Bahr al Ghazal to the far reaches of the Ethiopian and Ugandan borders with Sudan, have very fluid alliances that can be established or broken over a truckload of grain. It is difficult to know who is fighting whom throughout Sudan.

In addition, outside groups destabilize peaceful settlements in the region. One of the most notorious is the Lord's Resistance Army from over the Uganda border, known for its wanton attacks and wholesale rapes of women and girls.

Occupations

The main occupation of Sudanese living in the sparsely populated rural sections is agropastoral, or subsistence farming, either cultivating crops or raising animals.

Some farmers are stationary, using hand tools crafted by local metalsmiths to cultivate small plots of ground leased from tribal chiefs in return for a share of the crop. These farmers rely on seasonal rains to water their interplanted crops of millet, sorghum, groundnuts, melons, cowpeas, and okra. The farms are small in scale, usually no more than about 12 to 16 acres. The technique of interplanting ensures that a portion of crops will survive attacks of pests or disease.

Stationary farmers and their families live in *gotia*, more or less permanent dwellings with conical roofs, straight-sided walls, and pounded floors. On the very peak of a few of the roofs are symbols of prominence or wealth, such as a bottle, crescent and star, or wand with fringe. At the sides of some of these dwellings are brush *rakouba*, or open-sided structures with a roof, for community assembly, cooking, or eating.

Other farmers breed and cultivate animals for sale at the market or for butchering, such as cattle, sheep, and camels. The lives of such farmers are nomadic as they search out feeding grounds and water sources for their livestock. They live in settlements of low, Quonset-style dwellings, often covered with blue or white plastic sheeting. Their establishments are set apart by a little distance to provide enough room for privacy and separation of the grazing animals.

Even in an area vulnerable to desertification and being overtaken by thorn bushes, useful trees, such as the nabag tree, may thrive. Its fruit can be used for food, and bark is prized for a tea that is said to heal intestinal disease.

All Sudanese farmers, whether stationary or nomadic, have basic needs for health, money, children's protection, and schools. August and September, when malaria is on the increase due to standing water, are the worst

A mother and her daughter in Geles, an Arab village in Darfur where ACT-Caritas has provided wells and a variety of other services.

(Paul Jeffrey, ACT-Caritas)

months for cash shortages. Treatment for malaria is expensive—if it is available at all. Many villages lack the most basic medical facilities. Some serious illnesses mean certain death.

Some blame regional conflicts on land use, the primary difference between these lifestyles—the sedentary farmers versus the nomadic animal owners. But the truth is so much more complicated than one single cause. Water shortages, the fronts of the war, desertification—all play their role. : Like the infrastructure of Sudan as a nation, the agricultural economy of the small farmer has collapsed in the years of war.

Farming is the main source of income for the Sudanese, but there are other occupations. Some Sudanese work in the oil fields or other industrial jobs. Some work as tailors, blacksmiths, or traders.

Vulnerability of Women and Children

Nearly everyone walks in the rural regions of Sudan. One woman told UMCOR workers that she walked as far as seventeen kilometers to draw water. Women and children collect water in the early morning. In the evenings a visitor notices women carrying bundles of firewood on their heads using a *tumpline*, or headband, to steady the load. Twenty or thirty long, thin sticks of wood make up a load for an adult. Girls carry smaller loads. A donkey is a prized household possession because it can share in bearing burdens of wood and water.

Women and children are very vulnerable to injury and attack during these long treks. The government of Sudan does not release statistics but some human rights groups have reported on systematic rapes and attacks on the women and girls. Rape as a weapon has been used in several wars in recent times. Rape is a way for the attackers to perpetuate social control and even to destroy the opposing community. In Sudan impregnating a woman through the violence of rape has several immediate effects and a lethal long-term one. An immediate effect is that rape shames the woman in her own community. If she survives the attack, she may be blamed for "allowing" it to happen. If she becomes pregnant, her child is one whom others may not accept. In a culture where interdependence with the community and the family are primary, she may be shunned, unable to feed herself and her child. A woman bearing the child of a *janjaweed* militant, for example, is likely to be punished or humiliated. If she has to flee her home community, the rape will have succeeded in its purpose—to tear the fabric of family life apart.

Most reported cases of sexual violence occur around the perimeters of displaced persons camps. Every day, women seeking to carry out normal activities of daily life and livelihood, such as wood gathering, farming, or collecting grass, face threats to their safety outside camp boundaries. Yet documentation of incidents is very difficult to obtain. In the Muslim regions of Darfur, sexual violence is an extremely sensitive topic. The social stigmatization is harsh, and discourages reporting of incidents. There is a distrust of local authorities, who may dismiss any reports as false, or even as mere pandering for political gain to nongovernmental organizations working in the area. To make it worse, most women and girls are not schooled, and may not speak or write Arabic, the *lingua franca* of Sudan. This makes preparing a report of sexual violence all the more difficult.

The social costs of reporting an incident of sexual violence are compounded by the distances one must travel to reach the authorities. Harsh terrain and dangerous travel conditions prevail in the roadless rural areas. Competing militias that control the systems for justice may appoint advisers and judges who may have no appropriate training in basic protections for either victims or perpetrators.

During Southern Sudan's twenty-year civil war, women and girls often could not outrun armed combatants as they descended on their villages. Many women and girls were raped and then abducted. Many were killed outright. Today there are still many dangers posed by armed bandits and opportunistic criminals for women and children in the South as the displaced and refugees return from camps in Kenya and Ethiopia.

Women in these conflict-torn areas are particularly vulnerable to abuses of their rights. The United Nations High Commissioner for Human Rights cited both the government of Sudan and other armed militia units for their war strategy of rape, attempted rape, and committing other forms of sexual and gender-based violence against women and girls. The UNHCHR documented a number of these incidents reported by survivors who reported resisting but then were unable to overcome the physical force and humiliations of the perpetrators.

In another report called "Five Years On," Human Rights Watch observers detailed the range of sexual violence occurring in Sudan, particularly in Darfur. Human Rights Watch is an international organization that produces briefing papers and reports on human rights situations around the globe. Though the pattern of government and militia attacks has subsided recently, the number of competing militias, armed government military combatants, and armed bandits has increased the danger and vulnerability for women and children. Military, militia, police, rebels, former rebels, and criminal gangs are all involved.

Child Soldiers:

Children have been kidnapped and pressed into service as "child soldiers." A child soldier may have various roles in accompanying his or her kidnappers—cook, runner, and baggage-carrier are some of the safer assignments. Sexual slavery is rampant among the children so removed from home.

A Primer on Islam

The word Islam can mean "surrender" or "peace." So it is a terrible irony that a country that counts so many devout Muslims among its citizens must suffer so in a seemingly never-ending war. The faith of Islam and its influence in the world in general and in Sudan in particular has often been difficult for Westerners to understand. From its beginnings, Islam inspired fear and prejudice among many Christians. Recently Islam has been characterized by many Americans and sometimes by the Western media, as merely extremist or funda-mentalist, leading to frightening violence and intoler-ance. A perceived prejudice in the Western response to the humanitarian tragedy in Sudan may underlie this characterization of Islam.

Yet most of the world's billion Muslims—including the estimated 29 million to 37 million in Sudan—practice a faith that is moral, disciplined, direct, justice-oriented, and peace-loving. The following is a short primer on the faith of Islam. The sidebar on p. 29 contains a few suggestions for readers who want to explore Islam more deeply.

Islam is based on the revelation of God in the 7th cen-tury to the religious visionary Muhammad, whom Mus-lims revere as the last prophet of God. Muhammad is believed to have recorded these messages verbatim in a form that came to be known as the Qur'an, or holy book of Islam. The word Qur'an means "revelation." Originally published in Arabic, the Qur'an is now avail-able in most of the world's languages.

From the teachings of the Qur'an, Muslims identify five elements of faith that constitute the foundational beliefs of Islam. Breathing life into the five beliefs are five prac-tices, or pillars; responsibilities that every adult Muslim is expected to perform.

The Five Articles of Faith

Faith in God

The most important of the elements of faith is the belief in the centrality of God—and in the distinct and unar-guable difference between God and human. Like Chris-tianity and Judaism, the other faiths of the Abrahamic tradition, Islam is monotheist. For monotheists, God alone is the creator and sustainer of the universe and all that is in it. Unlike Christians, though, for Muslims God is unique among beings and has no other form but God.

Faith in Angels

For Muslims, angels are as real as the divine God and creator—and play a role in the life of human beings. The Qur'an came to Muhammad through the angel Gabriel, and other angels are mentioned in the Qur'an.

Faith in God's Messengers

Though Muhammad is considered by Muslims to be the last of the prophets, Muslims believe that God sent com-munications to humanity through various messengers before God's final communication with Muhammad. Among the messengers and prophets acknowledged by the Qur'an are Abraham, Moses, and Jesus. Though not considered divine by Muslims, Jesus is believed to have been the greatest prophet and messenger before Mu-hammad. So important is the concept that Muhammad was the final prophet that it is heresy for any Muslim to claim the title of prophet.

Faith in the Holy Books

Muslims refer to Jews and Christians as "the people of the Book," because the Qur'an explicitly states that God's revelation came to both through the sacred texts of both traditions. When read side by side, the messages of all these texts can be understood as essentially the same: doing good, loving justice, honoring God, serving those less fortunate.

Faith in the Day of Resurrection and Judgment

The Qur'an's message of the uniqueness of God is paired with its message of a future day of judgment, when the actions of all human beings will be evaluated by God. In this belief the idea of personal responsibility and com-munity responsibility of Islam is most vividly upheld. In the call to account, God will resurrect all bodies and join them to their souls. It will be an occasion of trumpets sounding, and of each person's receiving his or her "book of deeds." If the book is put into one's right hand, the person's reunited body and soul will rest near God in paradise. But if the book is delivered to the left hand, the person will suffer eternal punishment.

The Five Pillars

The five tenets or core beliefs of Islam inform the practices of daily life. These Five Pillars, as they are known, are central to living Islamically. They are clear, simple practices, but so important that Muslims believe that at the final judgment one who consistently upholds and practices these articles of faith may be rewarded for a responsible, just, moral life.

Testifying to God's Oneness

If there is one Pillar that towers over all, it is the first: testifying to God's uniqueness and distinctive difference from all things human. This witness also includes an affirmation of the status of Muhammad as the last of God's prophets. Muslims are called to practice all the Five Pillars, but to avoid this particular practice is to place oneself outside of the community of believers. To become a Muslim one need only repeat the testimony, taken directly from the Qur'an and known as the *shahada*—the witness, in English—three times in a setting like a family gathering or at a mosque.

Daily Prayer

Devout Muslims pray five times a day, following the teaching of Muhammad from the beginnings of the community he formed. The revelation enjoined the community to worship several times during the day and at the beginning and the end of each day. The orientation is eastward, toward Mecca. The times for prayer are spelled out in the traditions called the *Hadith*. The times are at dawn; after the sun passes its highest point; late

Read More About Islam

"Why Sharia?" by Noah Feldman. Published in *The New York Times Magazine*, March 16, 2008, pages 46-51.

Islam in America, by Jane I. Smith. (New York: Columbia University Press, 1999.) The professor of Islamic Studies at Hartford (CT) Seminary offers a rich portrait of Muslim faith and practice in general and in particular describes the way Muslims in the United States live a post-9/11 faith.

Major Themes of the Qur'an, by Fazlur Rahman. (Kuala Lumpur: Islamic Book Trust, 1999.) The late Dr. Rahman was professor of Islamic Thought at the University of Chicago when he wrote this book on the content of the holy book of Islam.

The Holy Qur'an. English translations are widely available.

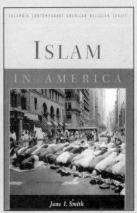

afternoon; after sunset; and sometime between sunset and midnight. Special considerations, such as combining some of the prayer times, assist those who are ill or traveling. Some Muslims living away from predominantly Muslim cultures may also combine prayers if prayer in the workplace is difficult or not permitted at all.

In Sudanese villages across the countryside, where Muslims are members also of tribal people who intermingle with those of many faiths, the call to prayer is given from the minaret of the mosque by a specially trained *mu'adhdhin*, whose gift of vocalization is seen as one of the great arts of Islam. In a bustling city such as Khartoum the call is usually a recording, amplified through a sound system.

Prayers are preceded with ritual washing of feet, neck, head, and ears. A visitor to Khartoum may note the tiled water points in each office courtyard. Another ritual sets the worshiper's intention and provides the transition from workaday activity to the heightened attention of prayer. In Sudan and other countries where Islam is a predominant faith, congregational prayers occur on Fridays. Women and men alike pray and attend congregational prayers, using separate facilities.

Muslim prayer is an activity of worship that involves the whole person—physically, mentally, and spiritually. Bodily movements, such as kneeling and full prostration, accompany the recital of prayers. Mindfulness about the direction the worshiper faces is part of the prayer.

Charity to Others
Caring for the most vulnerable members of the community is the third Pillar. Charitable giving, along with service to others, is a measure of a Muslim's faithfulness. The act of giving at one time was mandated almost as an income tax—the Arabic word for this is *zakat*, which means "alms tax." But today donations to charity are for the most part voluntary. Muslim projects include assistance within local communities as well as international initiatives.

Fasting During Ramadan
Ramadan is a monthlong spiritual festival that through fasting of many sorts celebrates the time when the Qur'an was delivered to Muhammad. Ramadan may fall at any time of the year, because it is based on the lunar calendar, based on the 28-day cycles of the moon. During 2009 when Schools of Christian Mission are studying Sudan, Muslims in North America will observe Ramadan August 22 through September 20. (In the rest of the world, the new moon will be visible a day earlier, moving the observance to August 21 through September 19.)

As with ritual prayer, Ramadan involves the Muslim physically, spiritually, and mentally. During Ramadan fasting occurs from the first morning light to the last light of day. During this period one may not eat or drink, engage in sexual relations, use rough language, or smoke tobacco. One must follow the strictest ethical codes at this time. All these expectations require a rigorous discipline that engages the whole person. It is said that when the evening comes, those who have fasted feel great thanksgiving for God's goodness as their senses open to enjoy the first light foods of the day.

Pilgrimage
The fifth Pillar is the once-in-a-lifetime journey to the holy city of Mecca. Up to two million people may be at the site of the pilgrimage at one time. The official month for the pilgrimage, or *hajj*, is the last lunar month of the year. Most Muslims who are able to participate identify the *hajj* as the singular moment in their spiritual life—a moment of great beauty, emotion, and awe.

The fixed end of this journey, where all the ceremonies take place, is at the Ka'ba, said to be a stone given to Abraham by the angel Gabriel. Worshipers walk in many concentric circles about the Ka'ba, as they reenact the story of Hagar searching for water for her son Ishmael. Perhaps you will remember that a well miraculously appeared, with God's reassurance to Hagar that Ishmael will be a "great nation." Some pilgrims—(called *hajji* or *hajja*) to be accorded great honors from then on—return to their homes with bottles of water said to be from that well. The story is in Genesis (21:8-20).

Christian Sudan

In contrast to the Northern states in Sudan, which are predominantly Muslim, Southern Sudan is often called "the Christian South" in Western media. Sudan is home to some two million Christians, and most of them live in the South.

Early Missionary Activity

Islam is the religion of the majority of the population, although Christianity has a long history in Sudan, beginning with the arrival of Coptic Christians from Egypt during the 4th century and Melkite missionaries in 543. Christianity flourished until the 14th century, when Islam dominated the remaining Christian presence.

Roman Catholic missionaries arrived in 1861, although their mission was largely destroyed during an insurrection in 1881. The Roman Catholic Church was reestablished in 1898, and the Anglicans followed the next year.

Missionaries continued to trickle into the country to provide medical treatment and education, with the goal of converting Muslims and people of traditional religious beliefs.

Read More on Village and Town Life

God Grew Tired of Us, by John Bul Dau with Michael S. Sweeney. (First paperback edition, Washington, DC: National Geographic, 2008.) John Bul Dau, born in Duk Payuel, Southern Sudan, paints a vivid portrait of village life as it was before he was forced to flee for his life.

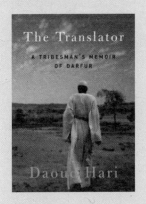

The Translator: A Tribesman's Memoir of Darfur, by Daoud Hari, as told to Dennis Michael Burke and Megan M. McKenna. (New York: Random House, 2008). Though much of Darfur as he knew it as a boy is gone now, the place lives in the memory of Daoud Hari, whose work as a translator for journalists such as Paul Salopek of *National Geographic* and Nicholas Kristoff of *The New York Times* came to international attention when he and Salopek were imprisoned in Sudan for some months.

The Translator, a novel by Leila Aboulela. (New York: Black Cat, a division of Grove Press. First American Edition, 1999). In the context of a love story, this Sudanese author has painted a picture not only of life in Khartoum but also of the faith practices of a devout Muslim woman.

Girls in Yei greet a visitor outside their kitchen.
(Michelle Scott, UMCOR)

Today, the Roman Catholic and Anglican churches are by far the largest denominations in the Sudan. There are also Coptic, Ethiopian, Greek Orthodox, and United Methodist churches.

The Sudan Council of Churches was established, with headquarters in Khartoum, in 1965 and includes Roman Catholic, Orthodox, and Protestant churches. It has an exiled wing, the New Sudan Council of Churches, based in Nairobi, Kenya. While the two councils see themselves as one, the many years of war and destruction have hindered their ability to serve together as an ecumenical resource for the southern Christians. In contrast the NSCC maintains regular contacts with the churches of the South, both spiritually and materially, helping with education, humanitarian assistance, refugee support, and spiritual solidarity between and among churches, all of whom, including the Roman Catholic, maintain close ecumenical ties in a fractured country.

United Methodist Churches in Yei

Before civil war broke out the United Methodists had established churches in Yei, Southern Sudan, through the activities of a refugee from Uganda. Today the Yei District of Sudan includes 21 United Methodist churches. Membership of each congregation is about 80-100 people. The district is part of the East Africa Conference of The United Methodist Church, which also includes Burundi, Kenya, Rwanda, and Uganda.

United Methodist mission activity began only recently in Southern Sudan, with the signing of a covenant in 2008 by Holston Conference and the East Africa Conference. Also signed by an official of the General Board of Global Ministries, the covenant established a partnership that hopes to build a school, medical clinic, guesthouse, teachers' quarters, and other facilities. In addition, the

The Anglicans pioneered girls' schools in both the North and the South. The African Inland Mission moved into Southern Sudan in 1949, establishing an outpost from its origins in what is now the Democratic Republic of Congo. The mission worked cooperatively with the Anglicans, and eventually established an autonomous church, the African Inland Church. When missionaries were expelled in 1964 due to civil war, the African Inland Church remained under indigenous leadership and expanded to other areas of Sudan.

partnership offers leadership development and school scholarships to church members for theological studies in Zimbabwe and Kenya, and to Sudanese orphans who attend a United Methodist primary school in Uganda.

Village Life
North: Ed Daein

Ed Daein is a rural town in South Darfur. Like many Sudanese villages in both North and South, it has a distinctive mix of low buildings made from blocks and covered with stucco tinted, like the earth around them, light reddish-brown. Walls about six feet high line the few streets, set in a grid pattern. A barrier of trash runs down the center of some of the streets. Cattle low under the shade of *neem* trees near a bit of standing water.

Many houses in the town are *gotia*, the woven structures with conical roofs covering circular walls made of rushes and twigs. They are said to smell fresh and clean in the rain, like dried grasses would. Most people live in compounds with extended family, and all the families know each other. Other houses are constructed of brick, similar to adobe, with tin or thatch roofs.

Ed Daein has one of Sudan's 85 airports with an unpaved runway. United Nations' flights land every day on the grass strip, occasioning the gathering of small groups of people to watch. The airport's control tower appears to be a reconstituted shipping carton. Visitors are told there is no working phone there. To one side, a tent shelters the little handful of blue-bereted African Union troops garrisoned at Ed Daein.

The cool air and pearl sky signal the end of the rainy season in August; the next day there will be brilliant sun over the trackless savanna. During the dry season a constant wind kicks up sand that gets into everything. A woman and a girl, dressed in yellow, peach, and bright green *taubs*, or robes, ride by on a donkey laden with sticks of firewood. They greet visitors with hands up in a most open gesture of welcome and vulnerability.

Boys and girls attend separate schools—open-air, woven shelters equipped with a blackboard. School supplies are provided by UNICEF, other nongovernmental organizations, or church groups. A teacher will lead the class through recitation of numbers or language. In Ed Daein, Arabic is the written and spoken language of the literate, though there are a number of tribal languages spoken by the several ethnic groups—Zaghawa, Massalit, Fur.

South: Near Yei

In Southern Sudan predominant tribes include the Dinka and the Nuer, both with ancient histories. Most people living around the Juba and Yei areas, where United Methodists have churches, are Dinka.

The Dinka traditionally have raised cattle and farmed. John Bul Dau, the memoirist who recounts his life as a Lost Boy of Sudan, describes the land around his home village as covered in eight-foot-high grass. The little footpaths linking one village to the next wend through the grass and around large stands of trees and forests of acacia trees. The farms in that area grow staples like millet and maize. A favorite food is *awalwala*, a paste made from millet powder and water mixed to a velvety consistency and heated. Cash crops like okra, beans, pumpkin, and onions supplement family incomes and diets.

The four seasons of Southern Sudan are a bit different from seasons in the United States. The cool season lasts from November to February. Temperatures typically do not fall below 55 degrees F. There is a short dry season in March. Then, during the hot season, from February through April, temperatures can soar to over 120 degrees. Rains come in May, moderating the heat.

During passing of the peace, Sunday morning worshipers at Yei United Methodist Church dance around their visitors while shaking hands. *(Michelle Scott, UMCOR)*

Hear the Sounds of Sudan's North

Sudan: Desert Rhythms and Savannah Harmonies. *The Rough Guide to the Music of Sudan,* produced by World Music Network, 2005. This album of desert rhythms has tracks that resemble the music of camp drummers and singers at El Ferdous in South Darfur.

These recordings have a way of reminding us that one day, peace and reconciliation might be realities in all of Sudan, North and South, and people will be able to return to their ancestral homes as so many of them say they wish to do.

Sudanese Music Online. The Smithsonian Folkways web site offers downloads of Sudanese music for a modest fee. http://www.folkways.si.edu/searchresults.aspx?sPhrase=Sudan&sType='phrase'

Dinka music online at Smithsonian
http://www.folkways.si.edu/AlbumDetails.aspx?itemid=757

Women's music online at Smithsonian
http://www.folkways.si.edu/albumdetails.aspx?itemid=756

Schools in many of the larger villages were destroyed during the civil war, and small villages may not have had schools or teachers. But village elders act as teachers of many lessons, both practical and philosophical.

The Camps: El Ferdous Models United Methodist Hospitality

On a braided track barely discernible from the floor of the savanna in South Darfur, a convoy of pickup trucks and high profile vehicles picked its way southwest from Ed Daein in the early morning. Each truck bore the white and blue flag of UMCOR, smartly snapping in the light breeze.

Headed to El Ferdous, the convoy forded several rushing watercourses and slid through beds of mud. At every bend in the track, every driver "hooted," or honked, to warn approaching vehicles. The 40-mile drive took two and a half hours. Stretching before the convoy: the eternal reaches of the Sudan savanna, a horizon unpunctuated by any landform, an almost unearthly green, a pewter sky.

"Humane" Reception Center

The displaced persons camp at El Ferdous and its host community have a total population of about 30,000. The camp is one of five where UMCOR has programs in this region.

The El Ferdous camp is a model of camp coordination for this part of South Darfur. The reception center, an UMCOR innovation, earned the distinction from the government overseer of humanitarian activities, the Humanitarian Aid Commission, as the only "humane" reception center in the Darfur region. Hospitality is important to residents of both host community and camp, who join together in welcoming visitors with dancing,

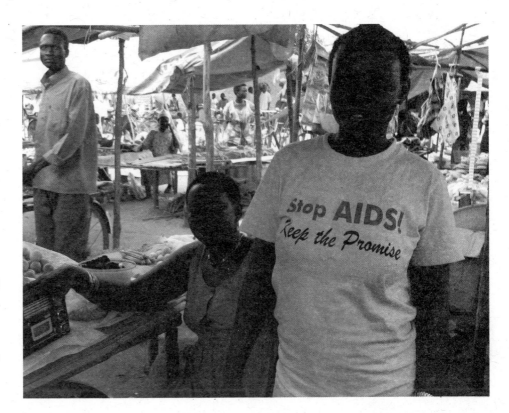

Thanks to UMCOR and Downers Grove (Illinois) First United Methodist Church these children now meet in a school building rather than this open air school.
(Michelle Scott, UMCOR)

chants, music, drumming, and speeches from community leaders.

A House of Their Own

Under a roof of grasses and reeds woven in a complicated diamond pattern, new arrivals provide information about their hometowns, their families, and their needs during the registration process. A leader shows new family members to the temporary *gotia*, or houses, inside a protected compound. They will live in one of the *gotia* until they learn where to choose a site for their own house and build a home using cut branches, grass, and reeds found near camp as well as plastic sheeting and mats from UMCOR. Community leaders also point out the necessities: water station, pit latrine, and food distribution area.

Since its installation in June 2004, the reception center has hosted some 20 to 25 households a month. Information collected at the center is shared so that the most vulnerable households can receive what they need not only from UMCOR but also from other international agencies working in the area.

Songs of Joy

It might be surprising to know that in a place of such loss and sorrow as a displaced persons camp, people can express joy.

But on the day visitors from the United States arrived at El Ferdous there was a festival. Everyone wore their best clothing. Schoolgirls chanted in unison: "Welcome UMCOR! Welcome church of Ohio!" (They referred to Ginghamsburg United Methodist Church, a generous donor for the sustainable agriculture program at the camp.)

The men, in pure white *jellabiya* and *ema*, the long robes and headgear traditional in this part of the world, drummed, while women in *taubs*—four meters of fabric tied at the waist and wound artfully around shoulders and head to provide a modest covering—sang and danced in time to the drums. The women also greeted the visitors with ululating—a kind of high-pitched yodeling originating deep in the throat and sung with fully open mouths. Ululation signifies happiness, celebration, and welcome.

Chapter Three
The Politics of War & Peace

The Politics of War

There are two recent wars to report on in Sudan. One, the civil war pitting the South against the North-controlled government, lasted over twenty years, starting in 1983, and killed some 1.9 million civilians. Women and girls of Southern Sudan were raped, kidnapped, and pressed into slavery to the North. Thousands of young boys and a few of the girls fled to refugee camps in Ethiopia and Kenya. They became known as the "Lost Boys and Girls of Sudan." The civil war ended when a Comprehensive Peace Agreement was signed in January 2005 by representatives of the North and the South. The comprehensive agreement—sometimes referred to as the Naivasha Agreement after the Kenyan resort where it was negotiated—received some media attention, but Western journalists had virtually ignored the war itself.

The other war, the *cause célèbre* of Western media, broke out in Darfur, to the north and west of Southern Sudan, in 2003. This conflict, now involving countless insurgents and counterinsurgents, has displaced some two million people and caused some 200,000 deaths according to United Nations estimates. Like many other aspects of the conflict, these estimates are subject to contest. In 2008 the UN suggested that the deaths may have reached 300,000. Sudan has countered with its own estimate of no more than 10,000 deaths. While celebrities and journalists alike have focused on this conflict, it has become increasingly regional and cross-border in scope.

The problem with splitting one war from the other is this. It distorts the complex interdependency of the whole of Sudan. In both wars guns and politics have had the potential to change the balance of power. A long-running political battle between Sudanese President Omar Hassan al-Bashir and Islamic scholar Hassan al-Turabi that has had such bearing on the situation in Darfur involves both guns and politics and is a case in point. Turabi was once a colleague of al-Bashir. He turned into al-Bashir's chief rival, when he was accused of backing one of Darfur's key rebel groups. Earlier, he sided with Saddam Hussein's incursion into Kuwait in the early 1990s. Though no supporter of Hussein, Turabi saw that moment as the one where Islamic revolution would sweep the whole region. In doing so he opened up Sudan to fringe militants from the Arab and Islamic world (including Osama Bin Laden, who had been stripped of his Saudi citizenship), and condemned Sudan to further isolation. The ongoing contest is a hint of the many complexities affecting Sudan's politics of war.

Possible Causes

Some Western observers of the scene in Darfur suggest that the basis for the conflict is animosity between Arab Muslims and so-called "Black Africans" or between nomadic people and agricultural people with fixed lands. But these suggestions oversimplify the reality on the ground. There is much manipulation on all sides—from the government; from recently converted insurgents, such as Minni Arkoi Minnawi, who now support Khartoum; from the anarchy of tribal clashes; from outside interests, not only countries bordering Sudan, but those who count on its supplies of oil, cotton, and other commodities. The destabilization of both Darfur and Southern Sudan seems to be encouraged by strategists within the government and their allies who resist sharing power and access to resources outside their own circles. Observers have identified four strands of issues that contribute to the breakdown of law and the violence of Sudan's Darfur region: climate change; a failed counterinsurgency; a deliberate state policy of ethnic cleansing; and the tragedy of colonial occupation.

Recapped here are some of the key details behind these four scenarios that can help Westerners to make sense of the firestorm in Darfur and its relationship to the whole of Sudan. The first three are based on Gerard Prunier's analysis supplemented with United Nations reports. The fourth is based on the work of African scholars Mary E. Modupe Kolawole and Ifi Amadiume.

1. Global Climate Change

The first is that climate conditions—especially drought— accelerated uncontrollable tensions among ethnic groups vying for grasslands, water, and farmland. This is often the explanation that Khartoum puts forward. When Abdalhaleem Mohamad, the then Sudanese ambassador to the United Nations, claimed at a May 2007 Reuters-sponsored forum on Darfur (attended by the writer) that climate change had transformed the geopolitics of the region, he was mocked by other panelists.

In fact, climatologists' studies of rain levels show steadily decreasing rainfalls, especially in the North. For example at Al Fasher, the capital of North Darfur, rainfall in 1976 was about 10.5 inches. In 1986 it was about 6.3 inches. In 2005 Al Fasher's annual rainfall was less than 5 inches. Climate change has shortened the growing season and truncated the life spans of animals counted on for trade and nutrition, not to mention the life spans of the people themselves. At the same time, population density has shifted upward in some of the most fragile areas. The resulting conflict has not only disrupted traditional livelihoods and destroyed knowledge of traditional environmental management practices, but has caused migrations of large numbers of people into regions already stressed by lack of resources. An 18-month study by the United Nations Environment Program concluded the same. Climate change is real. The Sahara is moving south, at a rate of up to 5.5 kilometers or 3.4 miles per year.

2. Failed Counterinsurgency

The second reason for the escalation of violence in Darfur is that the situation is an example of a counterinsurgency gone terribly wrong. In this explanation, the roots of the unrest extend far back in history, to the days of combined Egyptian and British rule. The alienation and marginalization that characterized that period for Darfur continue to mark the region. The power of the ballot box did not improve the status of Darfur. President al-Bashir's rival, Hassan al-Turabi, saw the potential for enlisting Darfur in a counter-government uprising and collaborated with the Sudan People's Liberation Army, which had fought in the South, and the Justice and Equality Movement, to that end. In 2001 his followers obtained weapons, Prunier claims, from both the SPLA and the Eritrean government. The Sudan government's overly harsh measures to quell the insurgency of these two factions, the Sudan Liberation Movement and the Justice and Equality Movement, failed. Since Northern government troops were still waging war in the South, the central government hired militia to further suppress the activity in Darfur. All parties rebuffed attempts at negotiations.

By July 2003 the violence took on a previously unseen scale. Bombings and sweeping a bombed area with gunfire and fire proved deadly for civilians in Darfur. When these scorched-earth policies began to be reported by refugees in Chad border camps, the Western media followed suit. Prunier writes in his book *Darfur: The Ambiguous Genocide*, "Part of the reason why the violence reached genocidal proportions was the climate of complete contradiction and political infighting among the various cliques within the government." He writes that the "horror is not a coherent horror"—meaning that the complexity makes it very difficult for Westerners to fully understand. The spoken goal of the government of Sudan, unity, and the actions of the government that lead to further destabilization in Darfur and coincidentally in the South, don't seem to mesh. Turabi, the Muslim scholar and lawyer, was released from house arrest in 2003. He was never brought to trial. Meanwhile, poverty, shortages of food, disruptions in the ability to sustain traditional livelihoods, and the war-related migrations of tens of thousands of people began to fuel genuine interethnic clashes among competitors for shrinking resources.

3.

Ethnic Cleansing

The third reason for the Darfur war suggested by Prunier—and supported by the July 2008 International Criminal Court indictment naming Sudan's president responsible for genocide and crimes against humanity—is that the war is a deliberate act of ethnic cleansing. In this explanation, ethnic cleansing in Darfur is the government's strategy for removing people from the region whose ethnic backgrounds (for example so-called "non-Arab" tribal people) might pose a threat to the hegemony, or total control, of the Khartoum government. The same people, marginalized for years, have argued for a share of the wealth that would accrue as oil, ore, and water are harvested—and, as goes this

understanding of the situation—the government does not want to share. New words like *janjaweed* came into the vocabulary of the West.

The first reports of militia, or so-called *janjaweed* activity, were reported in *Al-Yayyam*, September 2003. In March 2004 the United Nations coordinator for Human Rights in Sudan, Mukesh Kapila, called Darfur "the world's greatest humanitarian crisis." Kapila further compared Darfur to Rwanda, where he had served during the genocide there. As an explanation for Darfur the word genocide was picked up by Western journalists—who could understand the simplicity of Arabs killing Africans—and it was given luster by United States officials such as then-Secretary of State Colin Powell who told journalists in September 2005 that in his opinion Darfur was a genocide. Genocide as a concept became the basis of the revival or even the very existence of some human rights advocacy organizations such as the International Crisis Group and Save Darfur. That is the position taken by Daoud Hari, the writer of the memoir *The Translator*.

The December 1948 International Convention on the Prevention and Punishment of Crimes of Genocide describes genocide as "deliberately inflicting on the group conditions of life calculated to bring about its physical destruction in whole or in part." It may seem obvious that, based on this definition, what happened in Darfur in the early 2000s was a genocide. The United Nations found this not to be so. In its 2005 report, the UN commission investigating atrocities in Darfur found no evidence that the Khartoum government had a policy of genocide in Darfur, but its "systematic abuses" through attacks on civilians in Darfur constituted serious crimes against humanity. What is not much mentioned in the focus on Darfur is that the suffering in Southern Sudan

through its years of war may have also met the 1948
definition—had anyone investigated back then.

In 2008 it was unclear how these charges would play
out, in light of the fresh news of the International Criminal Court's indictment of Omar al-Bashir. The evidence
would not be weighed by judges at the court until sometime in the fall of 2008, and there was no consensus in
the international community about the harm or help
that the charges might offer to the people of Sudan.

4. The Tragedy of Colonial Occupation—A Fourth Cause

A fourth cause for the crisis not only in Darfur but
also in the whole of Sudan, is the tragedy of colonial
occupation. Considering its lengthy history—since bibli-
cal times and before—Sudan has been an independent
nation in contemporary terms for just over 50 years.
Darfur, now haunted by hunger and war, arose as a
powerful sultanate in the 14th century. Islam thrived
alongside traditional religions; the region itself was
known a nurturer of diversity. Of the 570 tribal groups
that make up Sudan's population, Darfur is home to as
many as 90 tribes. The Fur, still the largest grouping,

are indigenous to Darfur—the word *dar* means home;
Darfur means "home of the Fur."

Key ethnic groups whose ancestors migrated to Darfur
before the 14th century (that is, before written history
began to take shape) from the East are the Berti, Zaghawa, and Bidayat. Groups such as the Rizzeyqat, Ziyadi-
yya, and Ta'aisha are also early migrants from the East
and described as Arabs. In the 18th century a migration
of tribes from the Nile region below the border of Egypt
streamed in. They were termed "*Bahhara*," or "those of
the river," and their impact on the region over the next
hundred years was to monopolize the natural resources
and impose their own religion (Islam), language (Arabic), and administrative power. According to Gerard
Prunier, the *Bahhara* "in the South ... stood out as alien
invaders, but in Darfur they blended with the population as a nativized ... elite." Darfur was incorporated
by the colonial government into Sudan in 1916, to fend
off the possibility that the area would be incorporated
into the Ottoman Empire. But Darfur—considered by
the government a distant backwater of little economic
interest—was left with little or no investment from government, either colonial or liberated.

Here is the tragedy of colonial rule: it marginalized to
the point of silence the vitality and diversity of Sudan's
ethnic mix. It allowed the silencing of women, who had
enjoyed property rights and independence in their communities. Though the British intended to preserve and
rule through tribal structures, the effect was to virtually
destroy the leadership networks, decision making, and
judicial practices that kept peace among the many tribal
people and their often competing interests. And, most
devastatingly, colonial rule imposed an inferior status
on the indigenous people of Sudan (and of everywhere
else where colonialists imposed their European values)
that deliberately withheld education from most native

peoples (except the elite of Khartoum) and set the pattern for underdevelopment of the South and Darfur. Sadly, postcolonial governments in Sudan have not offered much relief from this approach.

As the British colonized Sudan, they largely ignored the South (due to its inaccessibility below the Sudd, or marshlands) and nudged the North toward "Sudanization," and this nudge led people in Darfur to abandon their own unique cultural markers, such as their tribal languages for Arabic, the independence of women, enjoyment of millet beer, and so on, to the stricter requirements of a less tolerant kind of Islam. "Sudanization" created a desire among some people who wanted not so much to be thought of as Arab, as of full citizens of the Sudanese state. When the British left in 1956, voicelessness, as Mary Kolawole calls it, had begun to seem like the norm for Sudanese women and men. The colonial powers made a show of weaponry, flags, and marching, to terrorize the people, in a "dominion by violence." Traditional patriarchy only heightened the effects of colonial repression. In the 1980s the people living in Darfur complained that their adherence to the rules laid out in Khartoum made them little better off than in the days of the British-Egyptian condominium (or joint rule).

Before Sudan won its independence, Britain and France had divided the old kingdoms of Darfur between Chad, then a French colony, and Sudan. After independence the Sudan part of Darfur was split into three states for political gain by elites from Khartoum, political Islamists, who could not win elections in any other way. This "reform" split the Fur people themselves into minorities in each state, sidelining their dominance over other tribal people and making way for them to be overcome in both elections and in the military sense. In the 1980s Muammar Gaddafi from Libya used Darfur as a base for military operations against Chad, with Khartoum reportedly turning a blind eye in exchange for weapons.

Summary of Key Issues

- **High intensity conflict.** Whatever the complex causes, the comprehensive peace agreements of 2005 and 2008 have not stabilized Northern and Southern Sudan. Conflicts among many disparate groups continue to harm civilians, the fighters, children, and even the government. These are continuing in spite of signed agreements.

- **Widespread displacement.** It is difficult to get accurate estimates of the displaced throughout the Northern and Southern areas of Sudan. The long civil war fought mainly in Southern Sudan until 2005 displaced millions. The separate conflict, which broke out in the Western region of Darfur in 2003, has displaced nearly two million people and caused some 200,000 deaths according to UN estimates. As of 2006, the year of most current estimates, all of Sudan's neighbors—Chad, Ethiopia, Kenya, Central African Republic, Democratic Republic of the Congo, and Uganda—are providing shelter for over half a million Sudanese refugees. Included are some 240,000 Darfur residents driven from their homes in the Darfur conflict. Sudan, in turn, hosted about 116,000 Eritreans, 20,000 Chadians, and smaller numbers of Ethiopians, Ugandans, Central Africans, and Congolese as refugees.

- **Destruction of livelihood.** Displacement not only destabilizes a region, but it also results in the destruction of livelihoods. More than 80 percent of Sudan's people, in both Northern and Southern Sudan, are crop or cattle farmers. The lack of access to basic necessities such as food staples, soap, firewood, and water has soared as a result.

- **Chronic drought and climate change.** The unprecedented scale of climate change as recorded in Darfur is one of the driving forces in ongoing conflict, as already mentioned and supported by a United Nations Environmental Program report in 2007. Poor rainy seasons caused by the changes in global climate in many areas of Sudan created urgent needs for food supplements. In addition the drought endemic to these regions, especially in the North, has created shortages of water for both people and animals and caused the death of precious livestock and the more vulnerable people, such as children and the old.

The World Food Program had to shrink its operations in Northern Sudan/Darfur in 2008, due to unaffordable prices and short supplies in addition to the dangerous conditions of banditry interfering with aid deliveries in the conflict zone. The warring factions may also be using food as a weapon of war.

- **Additional strains on resources.** In early- to mid-2005 some 285,000 people displaced by the 21-year civil war began returning to their homes. This included North to South and South to South return movements. These migrations placed considerable strain on the already resource-deficient communities in the South and in the transitional areas such as Abyei, Southern Kordofan, and Blue Nile states. Security of the returning people was also a big issue, due to militia activities, armed civilians, and land mines. When returnees arrive back home, hardships continue. Many remain without shelter, sufficient food, clean drinking water, and access to medical services.

- **Difficulty of consensus.** Gaining consensus on how to solve the many issues of land use, power sharing, and conflict resolution has been difficult to the point of catastrophe. So many different people, tribes, languages, economies, and stories are involved, and there is much blame for the atrocities and acts of war that some have labeled genocide, and others have called the worst humanitarian crisis in recent years.

Exclusion from Power Sharing

Another way to view the rebellion in Darfur is based in the over-centralization of Khartoum that has the effect of marginalizing the western province. Independence from the British did not change Khartoum's dismissal of Sudan's peripheral areas as backwaters that could easily be ignored. When the people living in Darfur realized they would be excluded once again from the wealth-sharing and power-sharing agreements emerging from the 2005 Comprehensive Peace Agreement, they revolted. Darfuri soldiers, represented in large numbers in the government of Sudan's army, could not be sent home to kill their own relatives. Khartoum, calling the rebels in Darfur *abid*, or slaves, armed the Arab-related tribes in Darfur with orders to kill, burn, rape, and destroy. The reference to *abid* obscured the real motive and gave Khartoum-controlled media a propaganda hook on which to report activities of *janjaweed*—mounted and armed militias— while disavowing their connection to the government.

The Crippling of Poverty

Drought also changes the balance of power. In South Darfur today, sand blows over the cultivated fields. Huge rainstorms carve the wadis into ditches. The animal tracks that serve as roads become impassable even for all-terrain vehicles. In 1985 with the drying winds of the desert came a flood of guns from Libya. These automatic weapons tore at the moral fabric of Darfur.

Crime waves went unstopped, though punishments for the criminals that were caught were savage: beheadings, crucifixions, hangings, mutilations.

Poverty crippled Darfur's people, perhaps especially the Arabs who lost animals to the drought. These Arabs also had the weapons, perhaps because they were more "Sudanese" (as described by the government) than the Fur, Zaghawa, and Massalit, the primary "non-Arab" tribal people in Darfur. The government began to recruit them as proxies for the military. They were armed fighters, and gave the government the cover of ethnic or tribal groups waging war against one another. Darfur has been called the battlefield for the power struggle in Khartoum.

Some observers, as noted in Chapter Two, have suggested that poverty in Darfur is directly related to policies of the International Monetary Fund and the World Bank. Baqie Badawi Muhammad stated bluntly in her essay on women's issues in Darfur that these organizations are imposing policies that "reshape and direct decision making in the country." According to a report to the IMF issued in 2007, the unity government of Sudan said the Fund had worked closely with the banking system to manage some of the economic issues: shortfalls of revenue, lower than anticipated oil production, improving transparency of reporting, and continued strife in both Darfur and in Southern Sudan. A news release reporting on a first meeting of the IMF with unity government officials conceded that spending on the alleviation of poverty had fallen short. During the height of famine in 1984 and 1985, according to Muhammad, the IMF did not support grain subsidies, and poor people were left to use their traditional handicrafts to generate cash, and to collect and preserve foods from the wild. Alex de Waal, the program director at the Social Science Research Council who has written

Food Preservation: A Creative Means of Endurance for Women in Darfur

Poverty in Darfur has necessitated creative and courageous responses among women to ensure survival. Baqie Badawi Muhammad has written that food production and preservation have long been the province of women in Darfur. "Food preservation was among the many modes of creativity that Darfurian women have utilized to develop and maintain a means of endurance," she said. Foods dried by women include meat, intestines, and fish. In addition, dried okra, tomato, and red pepper, meticulously preserved, supplement the diet, together with dairy products like *berkeb* (yogurt) and butter. Foods collected in the wild for preservation include wild grass, rice, and fruits.

extensively on Sudan, also blames the inaction of the pre-al-Bashir government of Gaafar al-Nimeiri for the scope of that famine and cites it as a leading cause for Nimeiri's overthrow in 1985.

The Myths of War

Many well-intentioned Western media analyses, constructed from reports on the ground from Sudan, have had the effect of creating a narrative that tells only a partial story. Oversimplification has stemmed in part from cultural misunderstanding and prejudice. But there are other issues—The problems of access, intimidation of journalists, and suspension of publication of some independent newspapers (such as the Arabic language *Al-Ayyam* and the English language *Khartoum Monitor*, cited by Julie Flint and Alex de Waal in their book *Darfur: A Short History of a Long War*). Some Western observers have challenged the conventional wisdom surrounding the conflicts in Darfur and the less well-reported long civil war in Southern Sudan, including the religious, ethnic, and economic factors that have driven them. Among these observers are Emily Wax, a reporter with *The Washington Post*, who has spent years in Sudan reporting from Darfur and neighboring Chad, and de Waal, the writer and activist on African issues. Summarized below are Wax's challenges, with additional viewpoints from de Waal, about the most common misconceptions. Viewpoints at variance and their sources are included to provide a taste of the complexity of the wars of Sudan.

- **The war is not about religion.** Wax wrote that the long-running war between North and South had religious undertones mixed with the drive on the part of the South to share in the governance of Sudan. She contends, however, that the war in Darfur is different. Darfur is about resources and who controls them— land and water, access to economic development and livelihoods, connection to political influence. The war is about the grab of resources by the most powerful from the least.

- **Darfur is home to some of Sudan's most devout Muslims.** Nearly everyone living in Darfur is Muslim—the civilian villagers, the rebel fighters, and the government attackers. Yet mosques are nearly always destroyed in the fighting. Alex de Waal concurs: "All Darfurians are Muslim," and he also suggests that long-lived tensions between ethnic groups, including groups who emigrated from Chad into Darfur because of drought in the 1970s, have contributed to the region's violence.

- **The war is not between Arabs and so-called Black Africans.** Everyone in Darfur appears to be dark-skinned, at least by Western standards, Wax writes. Sudan melds African and Arab identities. Especially in Darfur, these groups have been integrated through bloodlines and cultural assimilation. In Darfur—once a community tolerant of the contributions to the good of the entire region of diverse ethnicities—two decades of scarcity and famine have spurred conflicts between two groups of tribes: one whose main economic advantage are their animals, and one whose economies are based on farming. As Arabs began to dominate the centers of government and laws in the past century, it became politically expedient for people to call themselves Arab, no matter what their tribal identity. Tribes have intermarried for generations, but all sides have engaged in atrocities heightened by ethnic slurs.

- **The war may be in part about a long-running political battle between Sudanese President al-Bashir and one of his chief rivals, Hassan al-Turabi.** This suggestion of Emily Wax points to

A displaced boy does a handstand in a camp outside Zalingei, in Sudan's war-torn Darfur region.
(Paul Jeffrey, ACT-Caritas)

the complicated braid of Sudan's politics. A former speaker of parliament and college professor, Turabi headed—and continues to influence—an Islamist approach to reform and transformation in Sudan, according to de Waal. His former students lead a key rebel group, the Justice and Equality Movement, or JEM as it is known, that threatens the rule of al-Bashir. At the same time, Turabi appeared to be mentoring some of the leaders of the rebel factions in Darfur according to Wax. A former associate of Turabi's, Dr. Khalil Ibrahim, is chairman of the JEM. He denies JEM's continuing connection with Turabi. In testimony before the United Nations investigators charged with preparing a report on Darfur, he called the political battle between Turabi and al-Bashir "the main reason for the atrocities committed in Darfur." Dr. Ibrahim, a physician, also opposes the present national government with a vision of reformation that would strengthen Islamic values in government representation and decision making. The JEM, according to de Waal, rejected the Comprehensive Peace Agreement supported by the al-Bashir government, because it did not address continuing political and economic marginalization of Darfur.

- The war is regional and international, not simply local rebel groups fighting an autocratic government. Arming the government-backed militias are Chad, Nigeria, Cameroon, Niger, and the Central Republic of Africa. Chad, on Sudan's western border, hosts bases for Sudanese rebels, wrote Wax, and its present president is a member of one of the elite tribes of Darfur. A 2008 military coup attempt in N'Djamena, Chad's capital city, included fighters with Sudanese identification.

Farther afield, China is a huge buyer of Sudanese oil. China's state-owned oil company controls between 60 and 80 percent of Sudan's total oil production and is a 40 percent owner of Sudan's national oil company. US oil companies pulled out of Sudan during an unstable time when several oil workers were kidnapped by insurgents. F. William Engdahl, a commentator on the geopolitics of oil, claims that the US appetite to return as an oil power in Sudan is directly related to US policy to associate the government of Sudan with war crimes and thus pressure for regime change.

The connections of Bejing and Khartoum were well documented in Western media during the approach of the 2008 Olympic Games. China has assisted Sudan in resisting Western economic sanctions through its influence in the United Nations, and has not been especially assertive in softening Sudan to accept United Nations peacekeeping troops. China is not using its oil investments as leverage, said a United Nations official, Susana Malcorra, appointed in 2008 to oversee the UN peacekeepers in Darfur. Ms. Malcorra blamed the overall lack of sustained attention and coordination among Security Council members France, China, and the United States, for slow progress in Darfur. In another example, France, building on a long-standing interest in Sudan from its 19th-century military incursions against the British and Egyptians in the Nile Basin, may be using Chadian troops to fight a proxy war to gain some control of oil fields in the South. De Waal writes that Libya has supplied arms, purchased from Russia and China, to rebel

Lining up for water in a displaced persons camp in Darfur.
(Paul Jeffrey, ACT-Caritas)

groups and Sudanese government militias alike, using Darfur as the trade route for such arms.

- **The genocide label hasn't helped.** Wax's contention that the genocide label has contributed to the worsening of the situation in Sudan is supported by the United Methodist aid agency, UMCOR, which has taken the position that the use of the word genocide heightens the dangers to its aid workers in the region. Other agencies have concurred. In an August 12, 2007, essay in *The New York Times,* Sam Dealey, a *Time* magazine reporter, suggested that the word may derive from exaggerated death tolls and what he called "morality one-upsmanship" actually heightens the difficulty "for relief organizations to deliver their services." According to Wax, the genocide label seems to have hardened all sides in their positions. It has allowed Sudan to represent itself as the victim of anti-Arab and anti-Islam policies. The West, for its part, has used the label to fuel anti-Arab and anti-Islam feelings. It has allowed rebel groups to refuse to come to peace negotiations because they believe they will have the support of the United States in their own victimization. And, most unfortunately, the label has not spurred meaningful action on the part of the United States. The egregious misery of the people in Darfur is not only war-related, but also, according to the Center for Research on the Epidemiology of Disaster, due to disease and malnutrition that the war magnifies and heightens.

But the environment internationally is as complicated and changeable as the situation in Sudan itself, and Wax's point may shortly be moot. The International Criminal Court's 2008 decision to ask for a review of evidence of genocide and crimes against humanity committed by Sudan's President Omar al-Bashir shifted the landscape once again.

Resistance in Darfur

The Fur people, once the largest ethnic group in Darfur, were divided in the 1980s among three states, and are now in the minority in each of the states. The people who have been killed in the wars are of many ethnicities—the Massalit, Fur, Zaghawa, Tunjur, Kaitinga, Seinga, Berti, Jawamaa—as well as the Rizzeyqat, Arab tribal people. Rizzeyqat are local Darfur Bedouins. All Darfur's leading families have mixed ancestry.

In 2000 the Fur and Zaghawa organized the resistance to a government that is providing little development for them. The threat to Khartoum allowed the government to begin harnessing members of poor Arab ethnic groups in the western province as the state's proxy military.

The Fur/Zaghawa coalition soon became the Sudan Liberation Army. The Sudan Liberation Army may receive arms and training from the United States, among other Western suppliers, whereas the atrocities led by the Khartoum government are meant to solidify political Islam and fend off control by the West, especially the United States. The war economy, with stolen food aid, smuggled guns, and looted livestock, forces people to keep living in destitution and desperation.

Alex de Waal bluntly states that for President al-Bashir, peace appears to mean subjugation. De Waal offers evidence that al-Bashir's government is now employing political means, like stacking the local elections with pro-al-Bashir candidates, stripping people who once governed themselves to mere underclasses. He may be masking these strategies in the guise of rebuilding infrastructure and restoring people to their lands. However, seen from his point of view, the actions of the government are meant to stabilize a situation being roiled by outside interests.

Displaced women collect water at a combination deep well and 20,000 liter bladder provided by ACT-Caritas in the Ardabba IDP Camp near Garsila.

(Paul Jeffrey, ACT-Caritas)

Human Rights Disaster

There is no doubt, through whatever lens one peers, that a humanitarian and human rights disaster has been unfolding in Darfur. And no matter how it is labeled the misery of the innocent civilians, women, and children, who have been displaced, requires action and follow through on an international scale. Following are the steps suggested by Juan E. Méndez, who has dedicated his legal career to the defense of human rights. The former United Nations special advisor on the prevention of genocide, Mr. Méndez wrote for Amnesty USA, stating these needs:

• Protection, including armed contingents to stand in the way of those who might attack defenseless civilian populations.

• Humanitarian relief, since those same populations are vulnerable not only to physical attack but to conditions of life designed to produce their extinction as a group. Also it is important to revert the consequences of previous attacks by facilitating the return of internally displaced persons to their places of origin.

• Accountability for crimes already committed, both as a way to generate trust among the population we need to protect and also to discourage new attacks.

• Addressing root causes of the conflict and not merely silencing the guns but bringing peace with justice. This is an important point when considering how to untangle the international implications of the struggle such as the economics of food, oil, and arms.

Of the prolonged conflict in Darfur, Professor Daria Nalecz, chair of the task force for International Cooperation on Holocaust Education, Remembrance, and Research, wrote to Mr. Méndez: "The international community certainly must increase its efforts to halt the ongoing atrocities in Darfur...especially those with an ethnic dimension." A report issued by the United Nations High Commissioner for Human Rights on "The Human Rights Situation in Sudan" concurred. It highlighted large attacks by government forces, sexual and gender-based violence by both government forces and the rebel groups, and the government's failure to protect its citizens as overshadowing progress in a peace

A girl living in a camp for internally displaced persons outside Kubum, in Sudan's violence-plagued Darfur region.
(Paul Jeffrey, ACT-Caritas)

process. The report further stated that such crimes must be mapped out and those responsible brought to justice.

The Grab for Resources

Through yet another lens, the wars of Sudan may be about resources and their control. Nowhere in the world is the grab by the powerful for resources of the less powerful more obvious than on the continent of Africa. If one truism could be identified about Africa's relationship with the rest of civilization, it would be that people come to African countries to take something from them—usually their wealth. *Sad !*

One need only recall the private fiefdom that Congo became for the king of Belgium, the gas fields of Nigeria being operated by multinational corporations without regard for the environmental harm caused by tarry smoke of burned-off gas, and the bauxite mines of the Democratic Republic of Congo and the digging of their tons of ore carried on the backs of ill-paid or unpaid children. These are realities in the last century and the present, and Sudan is not exempt from this grab.

In the fertile South, especially along the well-watered Nile Basin, are enough hectares to feed the whole country. Yet the land, torn and bruised by decades of war, barely supports subsistence farming though reliable rains keep many trees green year-round. Mechanized farms have taken control of traditional lands away from farmer-owners and put it into government and investor hands. Control of the southern oil fields has been one of the agendas for all the fighting groups, including the government. The war also destroyed whatever infrastructure was available. Schools, wells, homes, and community buildings are all but in ruins. In a country the size of France, there are only about 2,600 miles of paved roads. By contrast, Khartoum and Darfur are in the much poorer North—poorer, that is, in natural resources.

The underground lake discovered recently in North Darfur is another example of how resources might be grabbed from the less powerful by the more powerful. One concern about this new resource is that the government might try to control access to who may use the water. Dr. Ferial Louanchi, oceanographic expert at Institut des Sciences de la Mer in Algeria, called attention to another issue. "If this generation uses it up, there won't be any left." This water wealth, like Sudan's oil, is not renewable.

The Politics of Oil: US Policy in Sudan

Oil is a key resource that the North does not have and the South does. The government of Sudan is clearly interested in controlling the flow of oil for economic purposes of its own. In addition Western economic growth was in 2008 still dependent on access to more oil reserves. And the oil wealth of Africa appeared to be at least one driver of United States government policies on that continent. Otherwise the policies of the United States for Sudan seemed meaningless, even chaotic.

Located both in South Sudan and in South Darfur are large reserves of oil. Once considered within the control of major US oil companies like Chevron and Exxon Mobil—Chevron abandoned its oil explorations when the Nimeiri government was overthrown and US oil workers were kidnapped—the oil of South Sudan is now being pumped through a pipeline built by China to terminals at Port Sudan on the Red Sea. Not only did China exploit the former Chevron oil fields, but Chinese economic investment in the pipeline enables China today to receive some 80 percent of the oil pumped in Southern Sudan.

Intersection of Oil and Misery

According to William F. Engdahl, an economist and writer about oil issues since 1977, here's where the idea of genocide and the idea of control of oil intersect. It is a most unfortunate and seamy intersection. It has nothing to do at all with the misery of suffering people. It has everything to do with control of the resource of oil.

Engdahl's argument goes like this. If the United States can effectively win popular support for the idea that genocide akin to the Rwanda genocide of the last century is going on in Sudan, then Washington could possibly win an intervention that could lead to regime change. Such a regime change would benefit US refineries. Economic sanctions are part of US policy to drive such regime change

Pipeline politics continue with the US-built pipeline in Chad, near the Sudan border, to Cameroon. Perhaps coincidentally the Darfur genocide campaign began in 2003, when oil began flowing in that pipeline. As the world's attention turned to Darfur, framed in the campaign as the first genocide of the new century, Khartoum's April 2005 announcement of discovery of a new oilfield in South Darfur that appeared able to deliver 500,000 barrels per day when developed, was lost among reports of celebrity activists calling for people of conscience to save Darfur.

In addition to oil, Darfur possesses oceans of underground water. The region and Southern Sudan are also rich in uranium and iron ore.

Other observers do not buy the oil argument. Rony Brauman, former president of Doctors Without Borders, a humanitarian and medical aid organization that has worked in Sudan since 2001, told the *Human Rights Tribune*, a publication of the Geneva-based Human Rights Council, that in his opinion oil is less of a consideration than is an Arab-Islamist regime being implicated in a genocide or in crimes against humanity. Politically, Brauman said, this characterization of such a regime is a "godsend" for prosecuting the war on terrorism that has preoccupied the West since 2001. Brauman's view recalls the preoccupation of 19th-century Europeans in their scramble for Africa, and especially their righteous indignation against Arabs and Muslims.

Multinational Issues

The Displaced

The effects of Sudan's nearly continuous fighting among government and opposition forces since the mid-twentieth century have penetrated all Sudan's neighboring countries. As of 2006 more than half a million refugees have found shelter in miserable camps in Chad, Ethiopia, Kenya, Central African Republic, Democratic Republic of the Congo, and Uganda—six of the seven countries bordering Sudan. The seventh, Libya, has filtered arms and other contraband into Sudan.

Trafficking in Persons

Sudan is a source country for children, women, and men trafficked for purposes of forced labor and sexual exploitation, according to the May 2008 online version of the *CIA Fact Book*. Boys are spirited away to the Middle East, especially to Qatar and the United Arab Emirates, for use as camel jockeys. Small numbers of girls may be trafficked within Sudan for domestic servitude as well as for sexual exploitation. The Uganda-based Lord's Resistance Army abducts and forcibly conscripts young children in Southern Sudan for use as combatants in its ongoing war with the Uganda government.

It is difficult to determine the numbers of people affected. State Department estimates (in the 2007 Trafficking of Persons report) are stated in the amorphous "thousands," since Sudan's government recognizes only child soldiers as trafficked persons. According to the report the governments of Northern and Southern Sudan together claimed to have demobilized 721 child soldiers, including 18 in Darfur, in 2006 (the most current data at this writing), but no outside sources had verified the claim. During the decades of the civil war thousands of Dinka women and children were enslaved by people referred to as *Baggara*, or herdsmen. Slavery in this context meant forced labor on farms or in homes as domestics, as well as sexual exploitation. In 2001 a delegation led by Walter E. Fauntroy, who then chaired the Congressional Black Caucus, visited Sudan. In their independent investigation delegation members found likely evidence of such crimes. In Southern Sudan this form of intertribal trafficking appeared to have ended with the signing of the Comprehensive Peace Agreement. The government of Sudan has consistently denied these and other international accusations of slavery.

"No More Saviors"

Does the injunction to "save" Darfur find its impulse in a gift of caring deeply for the region and for the misery of so many, as Gerard Prunier, director of the French Center for Ethiopian Studies in Addis Ababa, contends? Or does it spring from something like the heyday of European colonialism, when missionaries were sent to Africa to introduce Africans to education, Jesus Christ, and "civilization"? The latter is the assertion of Uzodinma Iweala, author of a novel about child soldiers. Iweala's parents are Nigerians now living in the United Kingdom.

Writing in *The Washington Post* in July 2007 Iweala said, "There is no African, myself included, who does not appreciate the help of the wider world but we do question whether aid is genuine or given in the spirit of affirming one's cultural superiority."

The genuine aid called for by Iweala could take form as a result of the United Nations Millennium Development Goals, an initiative of the UN launched in 2000. The goals comprise a global strategy to reverse the effects

Comprehensive Peace Agreement Summary

Here is a quick summary of the Comprehensive Peace Agreement that was to have ended the 21-year civil war between the North and the South.

Sudan Comprehensive Peace Agreement (CPA), Signed January 9, 2005	
Provision	**Details of Provision**
Armed Forces	The North and South are to maintain separate armed forces. There is to be the withdrawal of 91,000 government troops from the South within two and a half years. The Sudan People's Liberation Army (SPLA) has eight months to withdraw its forces from the North. If, after the interim period the South decides not to secede, both sides will unify into a 39,000 strong force.
Autonomy	The South will have autonomy for six years to be followed by a referendum in 2011 regarding secession from the Khartoum government.
Oil Wealth	To be shared equally between the Khartoum government and the SPLA.
Economic Issues	Two separate currencies are to be used within a dual banking system. The North will retain the Sudanese pound while the South will opt for the Sudanese dinar. Essentially, the dual banking system means that banks will be commonly stationed with two different windows for service.
Administration	Positions in the central, transitional government are to be split 70:30 in favor of the Khartoum government, and 55:45 in favor of the government in the contentious areas of Abyei, the Blue Nile State, and the Nuba Mountains. Omar Hassan al-Bashir's position as Head of State is entrenched and John Garang (killed in July 2005; replaced with Salva Kiir) is to serve as vice president. A government of national unity is to be formed.
Islamic Law	Sharia is to remain applicable in the North and parts of the constitution are to be rewritten so that sharia does not apply to any non-Muslims throughout Sudan. The status of sharia in Khartoum is to be decided by an elected assembly.
Other	Each territory is to use its own flags. The North will maintain use of the current Sudanese flag and the South is to introduce its own flag.

of extreme poverty. One of the foci of the goals is sub-Saharan Africa as a region where such aims as eradication of poverty and hunger, reduction of child mortality, achievement of gender equality, and universal primary education could have, in the most positive sense, a "saving" effect through self-transformation aided by international development investments.

But Iweala objects to the West using Africa as the site for their "redemption." It's that oft-repeated pattern of the powerful taking from the weak, and in this case it is the powerful using the people of Africa as props for a savior-of-the-world fantasy. "I hope people will realize Africa doesn't want to be saved," wrote Iweala. "Africa wants the world to acknowledge that through fair partnerships with other members of the global community, we ourselves are capable of unprecedented growth."

Goal Eight of the Millennium Development Goals may approach those "fair partnerships" being called for by Iweala. A report, "Investing in Development: A Practical Plan to Achieve the Millennium Development Goals," was completed by the UN in 2005. Though Sudan itself was not included among the countries selected for piloting strategies of the program (because of its yet unstable situation), the eight goals themselves are worthy aspirations. In addition to the global partnership goal mentioned above, Millennium Development Goals include improving maternal and child health, combating HIV/AIDS, ensuring environmental sustainability, fostering universal education and gender equality, and ending hunger and poverty. The time frame now is 2015. Implementers in 2008 are blaming the slow progress in the sub-Saharan region on the very real issues of government instability (and inconsistent cooperation), war, and displacement.

Iweala and other observers like him will not accept the goals as good for Africa if they are merely the dreams of celebrities and industrialized nations. The people saving Africa, he wrote, are the social workers, negotiators, and indigenous humanitarian aid workers who are doing "incredible work" to fix the problems of their continent and their homelands.

The Problem With the Peace Agreement

The problem with the 2005 peace agreement is that it is neither comprehensive nor a consensus, according to critics such as Adam M. Mousa Midibo, who in 2008 was vice-chair of the opposition Umma Party. Though the Umma is Sudan's largest political party, it was not a signatory of the 2005 agreement. He told a reporter in 2006 that the agreement "does not reflect the ideas of the popular consensus of the Sudanese people. It doesn't change any basic facts about political life in Sudan." Darfur, out on the periphery of Sudan, was not part of the 2005 accord either. As the reporter noted, "rather than becoming a democratic, open society with a booming economy based on Sudan's oil reserves and other natural resources, as envisioned in the peace agreement, Sudan found itself [in May 2006] at the top of *Foreign Affairs* magazine's failed state index." The Darfur Peace Agreement, signed in May 2006 by only one of the guerrilla movements, failed as a robust guarantee of peace. Prunier bluntly called that "a weak paper bulwark against a harsh reality."

Chapter Four
The Dream of Peace

Politics of Peace and Reconciliation in Sudan

Just as the politics of war are complicated, so are the politics of peace. But there is a dream of peace shared by all sides in Sudan and Southern Sudan. It often takes the form of an expressed wish to return to ancestral homelands, to reunite with "those we left behind," in the words of an internally displaced woman now farming in South Darfur. What would it take to achieve this hope? And how can people of faith contribute to these hopes and dreams?

There are many agendas to satisfy, with none aligned to alleviate the suffering of displaced, wounded civilians in Southern Sudan or Darfur. The multiple opposition factions to the unity government; the shifting loyalties of oppositional groups and political parties, recognized and unrecognized; the interests, fortunes, and fears of neighboring countries; the self-interest of international trading partners—all present complex issues for conversation. Resolution will not be at all easy.

Here is an example. Only two political parties of the many in Sudan are included in the "government of national unity," as the government of Sudan calls itself: the National Congress Party, led by President al-Bashir; and the Sudan People's Liberation Movement, led by Southern Sudan's Salva Mayardit Kiir.

Many others that were excluded vie for power, wealth, and influence, including elements of the National Alliance and factions of the Democratic Union Party (led by Muhammad Uthman al-Mirghani); the Umma Party (formerly led by former prime minister Sadiq Siddiq al-Mahdi and in 2008 by Adam Mousa Midibo); the Popular Congress Party (led by Hassan Abdallah al-Turabi, the longtime rival of President al-Bashir); and the Justice and Equality Movement in Darfur (led by Khalil Ibrahim). The suspicions of the opposition factions that are not named in the unity government create layers of complexity. It is difficult to know who is on whose side, not to mention the differing ideals, agendas, and objectives of each one.

These competing parties, at least in Darfur, are being "watched over" by a comparatively small peacekeeping force. In 2005 when an UMCOR delegation visited South Darfur the number of African Union peacekeepers in the entire Darfur region (about the size of Texas) stood at only around 2,400. In 2008, pressure from the United Nations and the international community led to the increase of this number. As many as 26,000 peacekeeping personnel are planned in the United Nations Mission in the Sudan; its hybrid (a combination of UN and African Union troops), United Nations Mission in Darfur, has fielded about 10,000 peacekeepers of a planned 26,000 there. These missions are commonly known by their acronyms, UNAMIS and UNAMID.

Why Peace in Sudan Is a Theological Imperative

People of faith have a vested interest in peace for Sudan. Over the centuries our prophets and teachers have emphasized the value of peace as a marker for how God intends God's people to live. "So far as it depends on you," said the Apostle Paul in his letter to the Romans, "live peaceably with all." Muslims also follow a religion of peace, mercy, and forgiveness. The vast majority have nothing to do with violent events that some have associated with Muslims. In fact, persons committing acts of violence are breaking the laws of Islam.

Christians also believe that Jesus Christ's saving grace promises a climate of abundance. Christians find it unacceptable that the powerful, wherever they live, might grab resources away from the less powerful. Jesus Christ is also a liberator of the poor, according to James Cone, the African-American theologian who is the Charles A. Briggs Distinguished Professor of Systematic Theology at Union Theological Seminary in New York. He affirms, with United Methodists like Mike Slaughter of Ginghamsburg Church, that "God is not indifferent" to human suffering and that God's justice will prevail over the disorder of chaos. Cone writes that God calls oppressed people into being "for freedom." That must be our shared prayer for Sudan.

But we must give "legs" to our prayers for peace there. In that spirit, seven templates or best practices that people and communities of faith are using to give legs to our prayers are listed here. These are ways that we can support and also employ to help foster a climate of peace and reconciliation in Sudan and Southern Sudan. They are listed first, with more details below.

Entry Points for Fostering the Dream of Peace

- Models from African Americans

- The Truth and Reconciliation model developed in South Africa

- The sharia model that may have resonance for Muslims of the North

- The humanitarian model developed by many aid groups including United Methodist Committee on Relief

- The partnership model, also supported by UMCOR and employed by locally sponsored mission initiatives such as Holston Conference

- The "Africans for Africa" model espoused by both the Lost Boys and Girls of Southern Sudan and also some natives of Darfur

- The international model, based on the United Nations Decade for Peace areas for action and the Millennium Development Goals

- The church's use of its moral authority to advocate with international governments and courts that work directly with Sudanese government leaders of both North and South is considered in the next chapter.

1. Models from African Americans: People of Goodwill Acting Together

Religion News Service reported in May 2008 that the Interdenominational Theological Center, a consortium of African-American theological schools in Atlanta, has urged black churches to take proactive steps to address the crisis in the Darfur region of Sudan.

"In light of our Christian prophetic heritage, we call upon you to join us in denouncing genocide and the sin of silence regarding genocide in Darfur or elsewhere," reads an "Epistle to the Black Church on Darfur" released by the center in mid-April.

The statement asks that members of black churches and other "people of good will" petition the United Nations to call on Arab and Chinese governments, who have diplomatic or economic ties with the Sudanese government, to pressure the country to halt genocide and crimes against humanity.

The statement also urges collective efforts to encourage the US government to provide resources to the African continent that will sustain a workable peacekeeping operation.

It calls for churches "to pray for cessation of the oppression and restoration of humanity" and to set aside an upcoming Sunday to focus on Darfur.

2. Models of African Origin: South Africa

A restorative approach specifically emerging from the African experience is the truth and reconciliation process. In 2005 Common Ground USA conducted a study on the impact of this effort in South Africa that did so much to bring resolution to people who had survived decades of apartheid. It may be that the truth and reconciliation model could be adapted in Sudan, once a truly comprehensive peace agreement is created and then honored by all parties. Common Ground produced a report, summarized here.

In the last few years, the report points out, reconciliation has become one of the hottest topics in the increasingly hot field of conflict resolution. It refers to a large number of activities that help turn the temporary peace of an agreement which ends the fighting into a lasting end to the conflict itself. Through reconciliation and the related processes of restorative and/or transitional justice, parties to the dispute explore and overcome the

pain brought on during the conflict and find ways to build trust and live cooperatively with each other.

What Is Reconciliation?
Conflict resolution professionals use a number of techniques to try to foster reconciliation, with its components of truth, justice, mercy, and peace. These are familiar concepts for United Methodists and also for members of other Abrahamic faiths such as Judaism and Islam.

By far the most famous of reconciliation initiatives is South Africa's Truth and Reconciliation Commission. That commission held hearings into the human rights abuses during the apartheid era and held out the possibility of amnesty to people who showed genuine remorse for their actions. Since the commission's establishment in 1995, as many as twenty other such commissions have been created in other countries, which have experienced intense domestic strife. These projects bring people on all sides of a conflict together to explore their mutual fear and anger and, more importantly, to begin building bridges of trust between them.

Despite the violence in the region since 2000, some of the most promising examples of this kind of reconciliation have occurred between Israelis and Palestinians. For more than a decade, Oasis of Peace (*Neve Shalom/Wahat al-Salam*) have been bringing together students and teachers from both sides of the divide. Similarly, the Seeds of Peace summer camp in Otisfield, Maine (US) has served as a safe place for Israeli and Palestinian teenagers to spend extended periods of time together. Yet others have tried more unusual strategies. Search for Common Ground produces soap operas with conflict resolution themes for teenagers aired on radio in Africa and on television in Macedonia. Similarly, the clothing manufacturer Benetton sponsored a summer camp for teenage basketball players from the former Yugoslavia, one of many examples in which people have tried to use sports to build bridges, ironically, in part through competition. Last but by no means least, it should be obvious from the above that many people have used religion as a vehicle to help forge reconciliation. Thus, the Rev. John Dawson has made reconciliation between blacks and whites the heart of his 20-year ministry in South Central Los Angeles. Similarly, Corrymeela is an interfaith religious retreat center, which has spent the last 40 years facilitating meetings between Catholics and Protestants in Northern Ireland.

There is at least one common denominator to all these approaches to reconciliation. They all are designed to lead individual women and men to change the way they think about their historical adversaries. As a result, reconciliation occurs one person at a time in a long and laborious effort.

Why Reconciliation Matters

Reconciliation matters because many peace agreements, like those that have been attempted in Sudan and Southern Sudan, have not addressed the issues that gave rise to the conflict in the first place. If these go unaddressed to the satisfaction of all parties, there is little hope that the peace will be a lasting peace

Without reconciliation, fighting can break out again, as we have seen in Sudan. The report from Common Ground goes on to suggest steps toward truth and reconciliation that individuals, states, and third parties can take. However, it concludes, reconciliation is not a cozy solution. The process of former adversaries reaching true reconciliation through acknowledgment of painful truths can be not only cathartic for all sides but also perhaps in some ways as unbearable as the truth itself.

What Individuals Can Do

At the most basic level, reconciliation is all about individuals. It cannot be forced on people. They must decide on their own whether to forgive and reconcile with their one-time adversaries.

What States Can Do

By its very nature, reconciliation is a bottom-up process and thus cannot be imposed by the state or any other institution. However, as the South African example shows, governments can do a lot to promote reconciliation and provide opportunities for people to come to grips with the past.

In South Africa, the commission heard testimony from over 22,000 individuals and applications for amnesty from another 7,000. The commission's success and the publicity surrounding it have led new regimes in such diverse countries as East Timor and Yugoslavia to form truth commissions of one sort or another. The idea of restorative justice, in general, is gaining more widespread support, especially following the creation of the International Criminal Court. And, truth commissions need not be national. A number of organizations in Greensboro, North Carolina, have come together to try to achieve reconciliation in a city which has been at the forefront of many violent racial incidents since the first sit-ins there in 1960.

What Third Parties Can Do

It is probably even harder for outsiders to spark reconciliation than it is for governments.

Most successful efforts at reconciliation have, in fact, been led by teams of locals from both sides of the divide. Thus, the Truth and Reconciliation Commission in South Africa was chaired by Desmond Tutu, a black clergyman, while its vice president was Alex Boraine, a

A boy at play in a camp for internally displaced people outside Um Labassa in Sudan's Darfur region.
(Paul Jeffrey, ACT- Caritas)

white pastor. Both were outspoken opponents of apartheid, but they made certain to include whites who had been supporters of the old regime until quite near its end.

The one exception to this rule is the role that nongovernmental organizations can play in peacebuilding. The Mennonite Central Council, in particular, has focused a lot of its work in Central and South America on reconciliation. The United Methodist Committee on Relief uses a model of hospitality and cooperation in its work in Sudan.

Resolution Isn't Cozy

Even though reconciliation mostly involves people talking to each other, it is not easy to achieve. Rather it is among the most difficult things people are ever called on to do emotionally. Victims have to forgive oppressors. The perpetrators of crimes against humanity have to admit their guilt and, with it, their arrogance.

3. The Sharia Model: Could It Offer a Way for the North?

We know that the imposition of sharia law on the citizens of Southern Sudan only inflamed resistance to a failing, frightened government. Yet without some of the common trappings—which are largely cultural rather than stemming from the Qur'anic law itself—sharia might be a solution to peace, at least in the North. Senior adjunct at the Council on Foreign Relations and Harvard law professor Noah Feldman has written extensively on Islam and sharia. Here is a summary of a 2008 essay on the subject.

No legal system has had worse press in the United States than sharia, the Islamic code of law. Westerners imagine its enforcement in decapitations, amputated limbs, stoning, or so-called honor killings for what we may think of as minor offenses. Ideas about these draconian punishments have found their way into memoirs published by people from Southern Sudan as recently as 2008 as well as in media accounts.

Yet for most of its history sharia law has offered some of the most liberal and humane legal principles available anywhere in the world. Is it possible that its richest and most humane aspects could be built into a model of peace in Sudan, where multiethnicities and multireligions must live side by side?

Sharia is best understood as a higher law—God's law that applies to rich and poor, men and women, the rulers and the ruled. For Muslims, sharia means no one is above the law. Sharia condemns those honor killings the Western media report on from the Middle East. It insists on equal treatment for rich and poor. It protects everyone's property—including women's—from being taken away. The wearing of the headscarf is not sharia, a legal rule to be enforced, but the manifestation of the socially desirable quality of dressing modestly. But outlawing the use of alcohol and other dietary restrictions are a part of sharia, as is lending money for interest—though benefiting from investments where risk and return are shared is not.

Sharia is based on four streams of understanding that sound a lot like the Wesleyan Quadrilateral: the Qur'an, or sacred text; the path and teachings of the prophet Muhammad; analogical reasoning; and consensus or traditional interpretations over the ages. Legal scholars, or judges, were the equal of rulers in previous centuries, and provided the incentive for a ruler to avoid living "above the law." No ruler with Muslim values would have risked going against God's law.

In Sudan, as in many autocracies, sharia has been put in place without the traditional checks and balances of the

United Methodist Committee on Relief

UMCOR, the humanitarian aid agency of The United Methodist Church, was brought to life by the 1940 General Conference in response to a world refugee crisis in China. Impelled by the call of Jesus to serve "the least of these," UMCOR has been dispatching workers to most of the world's hot spots and disaster zones ever since.

In 2005 UMCOR opened offices in Khartoum and South Darfur to alleviate food insecurity and promote livelihoods for displaced persons with sustainable agriculture programs. UMCOR has expanded its programs to include installation of water stations, training classes for women and young adults in displaced persons camps, and primary school classes for children. In 2007 UMCOR workers began building schools in Yei, Southern Sudan, in preparation for returning families who had been displaced by the war.

The agency's work is funded through donations of United Methodists—individuals as well as annual conferences and congregations—and grants from US government partners such as US Department of State Bureau of Population, Refugees, and Migration, and the Office of US Foreign Disaster Assistance. A key United Methodist partner in Sudan is Ginghamsburg United Methodist Church, Tipp City, Ohio.

Besides UMCOR, 15 other aid agencies reported working in Darfur and Southern Sudan in 2008 according to InterAction, the trade association of nongovernmental organizations. In addition to secular NGOs they include denominational groups such as Adventist Development and Relief Agency, Catholic Relief Services, and Lutheran World Relief; and denominational alliances such as Action by Churches Together and Church World Service.

judges, whose traditional work was to hold the ruler accountable to the law. In the days before our 21st-century dictatorships and theocracies, Islamic law had the advantage of ensuring that ordinary people's rights were respected equally with the rights of the ruler. Today, executives of governments without strong judges may dominate without regard to these checks and balances, while the judge role is virtually powerless, relegated to family matters.

The imposition of sharia on the people of Sudan was seen as provocative by its Christian and animist minorities in the South. The Sudan People's Liberation Army mobilized some of its fighters around the ideals of religious tolerance and freedom.

The peace agreement of 2005 adjusted the application of the law so that sharia became the basis for the rule of law only for Sudanese in the North. The problem still remains that without checks and balances of the traditional judges, sharia as interpreted in Sudan may still allow government leaders to live above the law.

4. The Humanitarian Model

United Methodist Committee on Relief workers are among some 13,000 humanitarian aid workers located in Sudan in 2008. As the United Methodist faith-based nongovernmental organization, UMCOR has consistently demonstrated how people of goodwill can work together for the good of the whole population. Since its initial days in South Darfur in February 2005 and its opening of offices in Yei in 2006, UMCOR has been a model of peacemaking and diplomacy.

The staff, for example, is representative of many of the tribal and political groups showing up in the conflict. If there is discrimination between North and South in many social circles in Sudan, at the UMCOR office, "we are all Sudanese," Jane Ohuma, then head of mission, told visitors. Currently a number of Sudanese nationals work in the UMCOR offices in Khartoum, Ed Daein, and Yei. Jobs have always been assigned on the basis of merit, not on family or tribal connections, or on the basis of religious belief. For UMCOR peace and reconciliation begin at the office.

In the camps and host communities of South Darfur, UMCOR workers sought teachers for the United Methodist-operated child protection program from all sides of the conflict. Not a little accomplishment when one considers that in a single recent year the number of armed resistance groups splintered from around 14 to some 28. Children attend the programs, where they learn math, language, and other academic skills, without regard to their associations. They are simply vulnerable children who need shelter from the dangers of street life in the displaced persons camps.

Community leaders—elected from all sides—also work together to solve the problems of the whole group. For example they make joint decisions about who should be at the top of the list to receive aid. The UMCOR guideline is simply that the recipients must be the most vulnerable.

There has generally been no tribal violence in the camps. In 2005 visiting the camp El Ferdous, United Methodists were offered gifts crafted by the host community and by the camp community. Each group exchanged their gifts for the other's and presented the other's gifts in a show of cooperation and respect. Women, as leaders in the women's associations that are a leadership model in Sudan, were present at the presentations and added their welcome to those of the sheikhs and tribal leaders. We learned that women and men are active in the decision making about camp life and access to resources in the camp.

Water stations in camps and host communities now being refurbished or built anew are open to all people and animals needing water. There is no distinction between African and Arab, Christian and Muslim, pastoralists and nomads. There are simply people who need to be able to draw fresh, clean water in a place of safety.

The same is true of the skills-building workshops set up by UMCOR in the camps. Women and men of all tribes, backgrounds, and need attend the classes. New schools in the rural communities around Yei in Southern Sudan are being constructed for both Methodist children and Muslim children, as UMCOR works to rehabilitate the infrastructure damaged from so many years of war and neglect. Here is an example of that work.

"People's Need and People Driven"

On an August morning Jane Ohuma pointed to a large map of Sudan in the Khartoum office of United Methodist Committee on Relief. Jane's arm swept from West to East as she explained to a visitor the plight of displaced people out in Darfur, seven hundred miles from the capital city. Ms. Ohuma is head of mission for one of UMCOR's newest programs, operations in Sudan that began in February 2005.

Funded by a large gift from Ginghamsburg United Methodist Church, Tipp City, Ohio, and other grants, the agriculture program based in the Ed Daein region of South Darfur already had crops in the ground. Some 5,200 families were working the 4-hectare farms. At an average five per family, that added up to well over 25,000 beneficiaries.

A program like this is a bit like a puzzle. Needs and resources at a variety of levels, like interlocking puzzle pieces, must fit together. Most importantly, Ms. Ohuma stressed, solutions to hunger and livelihoods "must address people's need and be people driven." The United Methodist program does just that.

For example, to strengthen the local economy UMCOR contracted with local blacksmiths to make hoes and other handheld tools for the displaced farmers, rather than purchasing them from a factory. Displaced people have no land of their own. So area landowners offered parcels of land in exchange for a portion of the sorghum, millet, cowpeas, melon, okra, and peanuts.

An agronomist on UMCOR's field team showed the families how to "intercrop," or mingle, their plantings to reduce risk of crop loss to disease or predators. At one farm sorghum, groundnuts, and okra have been intercropped.

Good rains are also part of the equation—and when a delegation from UMCOR headquarters and Ginghamsburg church visited in 2005, they were excellent. The agriculture ministry of the Sudanese government predicted a bumper crop.

A successful harvest reaches into the future, Ms. Ohuma pointed out, providing enough seed for a new season, cash or barter capability, and sufficient food until next harvest. There is one planting season in Darfur.

Back Home: Uninhabitable

The displaced would like to go back home, said Ms. Ohuma. Instead they have joined Sudan's uprooted. For them, "back home" is uninhabitable. In Kubda, or Zalingei, or Muterr—towns in the Sudan's largest state of Darfur—the wells are filled in with dirt or fouled with corpses. All the houses were looted and burned, and schools and community health clinics razed. The people lost everything they had.

They fled in the hundreds of thousands in all directions—west to Chad, eastward and southward to the region of their state known as South Darfur. Some fled from the southern states. Now they live in settlements and camps for the displaced.

Their host communities, towns within short distances of the camps, are almost as impoverished as they are.

Some have fled more than one place, hoping for safety. Ms. Ohuma said, "The farms offer more than an occupation for those who are working them. They offer hope for their survival."

Setting the Standard for Other Programs
UMCOR aid workers have also constructed a reception center at El Ferdous, located in the same vicinity as the farms. Typically, said Ms. Ohuma, a camp population is rather fluid as residents enter and leave. The reception center allows a registration process that will facilitate

Fatna (right) brings home wood that she and some neighbors have harvested from outside a camp for internally displaced persons outside Kubum, in South Darfur.
(Paul Jeffrey, ACT- Caritas)

future UMCOR follow-up with the camp residents as they eventually prepare to return home.

The Humanitarian Aid Commission (HAC) and the World Food Programme recently named the reception center a model for all other camps, said Ms. Ohuma. HAC is the government monitor of all humanitarian activity throughout Sudan.

The farms are another kind of model. When new arrivals see "how beautiful the crops are," Ms. Ohuma said as she beamed, and what has been accomplished in a short time, they want to participate as well. HAC officials were also pleased at the rapid progress and extended the agency's mandate to work in Ed Daein for another year.

UMCOR is also distributing emergency supplies to camp residents. Plastic sheeting becomes a roof that provides shade from the sun and protection from the rains. Jerry cans serve as water collectors from the water points in both host communities and camps. Blankets provide warmth on the cool savanna evenings.

Originally from Kenya, Jane Ohuma worked for a time in Kosovo and then in Eritrea before joining UMCOR. "In Sudan there is so much to do," she said.

5. The Partnership Model—Two Living Examples

"Much to do in Sudan" is a mantra of one of UMCOR's United Methodist church partners. The Ginghamsburg church, with some 4,500 worshipers, has donated millions to UMCOR programs. The church—known among Darfurians as "The church of Ohio"—sent delegations together with UMCOR workers to camps in Darfur and government officials in Khartoum, and has hosted

members of the UMCOR Sudan management team in weekend church services. Here is their story.

I. A Church of Servants Contributes to Unique Partnership with UMCOR

Alex Applegate is ten years old. She's receiving $40 from her parents for her Christmas shopping. And she's giving half of that away to her church's Sudan project. Her pastor says such sacrificial giving is what servants of Jesus do. When a visitor asked Alex why she's participating, the fifth-grader responded, "Because it's the right thing to do."

In an out-of-the-way bean field near Tipp City, Ohio, giving is very much on the minds of Ginghamsburg church members like Alex every Christmas season. The United Methodist congregation has donated over $1.5 million (as of 2008) to United Methodist Committee on Relief's Sudan programs. They call it their "Christmas Miracle Offering."

"We're the Only Bank Account God Has"

"God is not disinterested or uninvolved in the world," said senior pastor Mike Slaughter during the sermon time in each of six services on a weekend leading up to the miracle offering. "God intervenes through God's people. We're the only bank account God has." A seventh service on Sunday evenings served up the teaching on DVD. Nearly 4,000 people heard the message.

Most Ginghamsburg families have not met the beneficiaries in faraway South Darfur. But they've seen the faces of children who can be kids again because they attend a safe school in the displaced persons camp where they fled when their home villages burned down in the war.

Jane Ohuma described the UMCOR school program, known as child protection and development, designed to shield children from early marriages, kidnapping, recruitment as child soldiers, and other forms of exploitation. In addition the 11,000 children attending the schools are from all sides of the conflict in South Darfur, as are their teachers. Such diversity helps to ensure the sustainability of the program. "When we are out in the field in South Darfur, we know there are people in Ohio who are praying for us," said Ms. Ohuma.

"We Can Make Their World Different"

UMCOR opened operations in Sudan with the congregation's initial gift of over $300,000. A program providing seeds and tools to displaced families in South Darfur took on a life of its own. In the first year 26,000 benefited and returned some of the harvest so that in the program's second year, some 50,000 are receiving benefits—food, cash for basic necessities like soap and sugar, and seed for the next planting season.

"The church of Ohio" experiences their connection to the people of South Darfur as durable. They believe they can "make their world different," in the words of one of the worship leaders, through their commitment and their action. They encourage world citizenship by showing not the desperation but the joy of people's lives. Photographs posted in the hallways, and a DVD showing the school in action, showed faces shining with hope. It's a hope shared by this church of servants.

II. *United Methodists in Yei and Holston Conference:* Rebuilding Together

Aside from UMCOR there is a Methodist presence in Southern Sudan, actively working for justice and peace in their region. About twenty-one United Methodist congregations, most of them established by refugees from Rwanda and Burundi more than a decade ago, are part of the East Africa Annual Conference.

This annual conference signed a historic covenant with Holston Annual Conference in the United States to build facilities and provide scholarships to church members and some children orphaned by the wars. It is the first covenant of its kind.

It started in the summer of 2005, when Bishop James Swanson and his staff discussed mission projects they could initiate. A photo taken in Sudan of a starving child being watched by a vulture, haunted the bishop. Within three years that historic covenant came into being, signed by Bishop Swanson and by Bishop Daniel Wandabula of the East Africa Conference, which includes Sudan. Bishop Swanson told the congregation at the covenant signing that "the salvation of South Sudan is my salvation."

A fact-finding team, including Caroline Njuki from the General Board of Global Ministries, went to Yei in 2006. What they heard distressed them, and then provided an opportunity for Christian reconciliation, according to Ms. Njuki. "Throughout the war the small United Methodist community in Yei felt abandoned by the church," she said. "They had never had a visit [from anyone representing the church]. When the war [in Southern Sudan] was over Darfur got all the publicity because the movie stars and politicians and media decided to get involved." The people asked the team, "Where was the church?" For two days the team, which included representatives from Holston Annual Conference, worked in prayerful reconciliation with the church members of Yei. In 2008 Holston Conference volunteers planned to be at work in Yei side by side with church members there, working on repairing schools and building a health clinic.

6. Africans for Africa Model

I. *Victor Chol: "Lost Boy" No More*

His name is Victor Chol. Today he's an American citizen, a soft-spoken college student in Maryville, Tennessee, majoring in international studies. Not so long ago, Victor Chol was one of the 27,000 "Lost Boys and Girls" of Sudan, separated from their parents due to the hardships and violence of war. About 4,000 came to the United States. Victor was one of them. The Maryville United Methodist Church sponsored his immigration to Tennessee and assisted him in finding a place to live, a livelihood, and a community. Victor has served as a resource for the Holston Conference.

Victor Chol was nine years old when his father was killed, and he and his mother and siblings fled Twic, a small village in the region around Waw in Bahr al Ghazal, Southern Sudan. "My father was a teacher in the missionary schools," Victor said. Anthony Chol was also affiliated with the Sudan Council of Churches, "and he was killed for his association with the church. We moved to the village of my mother." Militant factions of the Northern government, dissidents representing various political positions, militias of different strongmen, and armed thugs continued to "burn and burn," and to "kidnap and terrorize us."

"I Ran a Separate Way"

Soon, threatened with further violence, the bereft family had to flee again. They ran on foot. "I ran a separate way," said Victor.

For three months, he and others in his group crossed the tropical and desert landscapes of Southern Sudan. They crossed the Nile River, on their way to Ethiopia. "There were times we traveled in rainy and sunny days," he wrote in an e-mail.

"We were lucky," Victor wrote. "There are some who were attacked and robbed by rebel militias, but we weren't. I was following the crowd. We used to work in groups and when it was time to rest would select some among us to go to the villages to ask for food and water, and they would bring back whatever they were given and share with us. We did that to the point where there were no more villages and we had to depend on what we carried with us."

The Ethiopian border is many miles from Waw. Victor estimated that his three-month journey extended for 1,000 miles. He lived first in Panyudo Camp in Ethiopia. Then the children had to return to Sudan once again. From there they crossed the Gola River, marking the border between Kenya and Sudan, and walked to Kakuma Camp in Kenya. Both camps were facilities for displaced persons. Victor lost touch with others in his family.

"Thought She Had Forgotten Me"

Back home in Twic, Victor had applied himself at school, and he followed that principle at camp. He was selected to receive a scholarship. Officials at the camp isolated the children who did not arrive with their parents. "We lived in groups," he said, sharing books and materials. There were few textbooks and test booklets. "If you were lucky, you had a friend to send you a book." While living at Kakuma, Victor earned the KCE, the certificate of a primary school graduate.

Victor celebrated the new year of 2002 in the United States, sponsored by First United Methodist Church in Maryville, Tennessee, near Knoxville. When he was ready to go to college, he stayed on in Maryville.

"We organized a traditional dance to raise some money for refugee relief," Victor recalled. "My cousin came with other refugees and he knew where my mother was. I thought she had forgotten about me." Victor was working on his mother's arrival in the US when he learned of her death in 2005. Since then, Victor has served Holston Conference Sudan Action Team as a spokesperson on Sudan and interned in the Yei office of United Methodist Committee on Relief.

War for "A Handful of Corn"

Of the war, a Polish journalist wrote: "It is a war over a handful of corn, a bowlful of rice." Victor Chol concurs. Resources, economic well-being, power sharing and religion all come into play, he said. Southern Sudan has many resources, such as oil and minerals—its riches have been the focus of the much poorer Khartoum-led North. In addition, in Victor's opinion, the South has been marginalized for not accepting Islamic values prevalent in the North.

Dreams and Action for Peace

Some of the "Lost Boys and Girls" have created foundations or organizations to provide aid to their homeland. For example, Victor became the founding director of the Sudanese Lost Boys and Girls Volunteer Association in 2007 to use his education and experience to help rebuild Southern Sudan. That same year Victor returned to Southern Sudan for the first time in nineteen years to work at the Yei office of UMCOR. In 2008 he visited his home village, Waw, for the first time since his flight to Ethiopia and Kenya so many years ago.

Goals of the Sudanese Lost Boys and Girls Volunteer Association support the Comprehensive Peace Agreement and provide avenues for other Lost Boys and Girls to rebuild infrastructure back home in a variety of capacities, including education, health, and partnerships with other agencies now working in the country. Other goals are to:

Sudanese Entrepreneur Envisions Economic Development

Sudanese businessman Mo Ibrahim made a fortune in the telecom industry in Sudan. Now he has turned his business skills to creating an all-Africa initiative to promote good governance and development in sub-Saharan Africa. The Mo Ibrahim Foundation began publishing an index that measures the "provision of key political goods" in the categories of safety and security; rule of law; degree of transparency and corruption; participation in human rights; and sustainable economic and human development. Most importantly the index suggests these criteria as a way for citizens to hold their governments accountable. Mr. Ibrahim is Nubian. His own country, Sudan, ranked fourth from last across the five measures.

- Reintroduce traditional heritage, customs, and culture;

- Encourage and develop productive activities among returning refugees.

Victor's partners include the New Sudan Education Initiative, Holston Conference, the government of Southern Sudan, and the Peace and World Concern organization at Maryville College, where Victor studies. He has participated in a team to train youth in camps and small villages in the Yei area to connect with nongovernmental organizations as a way to serve their communities.

Other plans in 2008 included:

- New community center with clinic and dormitory at Juba;

- Borehole and well to ensure a safe, adequate water supply;

- Room and board for volunteers;

- Literacy and life skills classes;

- Recruitment and training of Southern Sudanese volunteers.

II. Duk County Rebuilds with the Help of Another "Lost Boy"

John Bul Dau, the Lost Boy whose memoir *God Grew Tired of Us* was the basis for an award-winning motion picture in 2006, has also formed a foundation to provide medical and educational services in Southern Sudan.

When he learned that residents of his hometown in Duk County had to walk 75 miles for medical care, he began fundraising. Land and facilities for a medical clinic were well on the way to completion in 2008.

Dau calls his approach "Africans for Africa," and encourages Africans living in the United States to become involved in philanthropic rebuilding. He wrote in his book that such connection can "appeal to the values of the indigenous people."

Like Victor Chol, John Dau is a man of faith. He was active in religious services in the camps he called home for 14 years, and when he immigrated to Syracuse, New York, in 2001 he was sponsored by a Presbyterian church there, where he continues to be an active member.

7. The International Model: "Peace Is in Our Hands"
(Adapted from UNESCO's brochure, "Mainstreaming the Culture of Peace.")

The decade 2001 through 2010 was declared the Decade of Peace by the United Nations. As we near the end of that decade, we can appropriate some of the action areas in regard to assisting Sudanese persons to find peace and justice in their world. The action areas are broad enough to gain a consensus across a wide spectrum of values and beliefs, and specific enough to suggest concrete initiatives for peace.

Following a proposal made by UNESCO, the United Nations General Assembly in 1998 defined the Culture of Peace as consisting of values, attitudes, and behaviors that reject violence and endeavor to prevent conflicts by addressing their root causes with a view to solving problems through dialogue and negotiation among individuals, groups, and nations.

The 1999 United Nations Declaration and Program of Action on a Culture of Peace called for everyone—governments, civil society, the media, parents, teachers, politicians, scientists, artists, nongovernmental organizations, and the entire United Nations system—to assume responsibility in this respect. It staked out eight action areas for actors at national, regional, and international levels.

Culture of Peace: Eight Action Areas

Education. Fostering a culture of peace through education by promoting education for all, focusing especially on girls; revising curricula to promote the qualitative values, attitudes, and behavior inherent in a culture of peace; and training for conflict prevention and resolution, dialogue, consensus-building, and active nonviolence.

Economic and Social Development. Promoting sustainable economic and social development by targeting the eradication of poverty; focusing on the special needs of children and women; working toward environmental sustainability; and fostering national and international cooperation to reduce economic and social inequalities.

Human Rights. Promoting respect for all human rights by distributing the Universal Declaration of Human Rights at all levels and fully implementing international instruments on human rights.

Gender Equality. Ensuring equality between women and men by integrating a gender perspective and promoting equality in economic, social, and political decision making; eliminating all forms of discrimination and violence against women; and supporting and aiding women in crisis situations resulting from war and all other forms of violence.

Democratic Principles. Fostering democratic participation by educating responsible citizens; reinforcing actions to promote democratic principles and practices; and establishing and strengthening national institutions and processes that promote and sustain democracy.

Dialogue. Advancing understanding, tolerance, and solidarity by promoting a dialogue among civilizations; actions in favor of vulnerable groups, migrants, refugees and displaced persons, indigenous people. and traditional groups; and respect for difference and cultural diversity.

Communication. Supporting participatory communication and the free flow of information and knowledge by means of such actions as support for independent media in the promotion of a culture of peace; effective use of media and mass communications; measures to address the issue of violence in the media; and knowledge and information sharing through new technologies.

Conflict Resolution. Promoting international peace and security through action such as the promotion of general and complete disarmament; greater involvement of women in prevention and resolution of conflicts and in promoting a culture of peace in post-conflict situations; initiatives in conflict situations; and encouraging confidence-building measures and efforts for negotiating peaceful settlements.

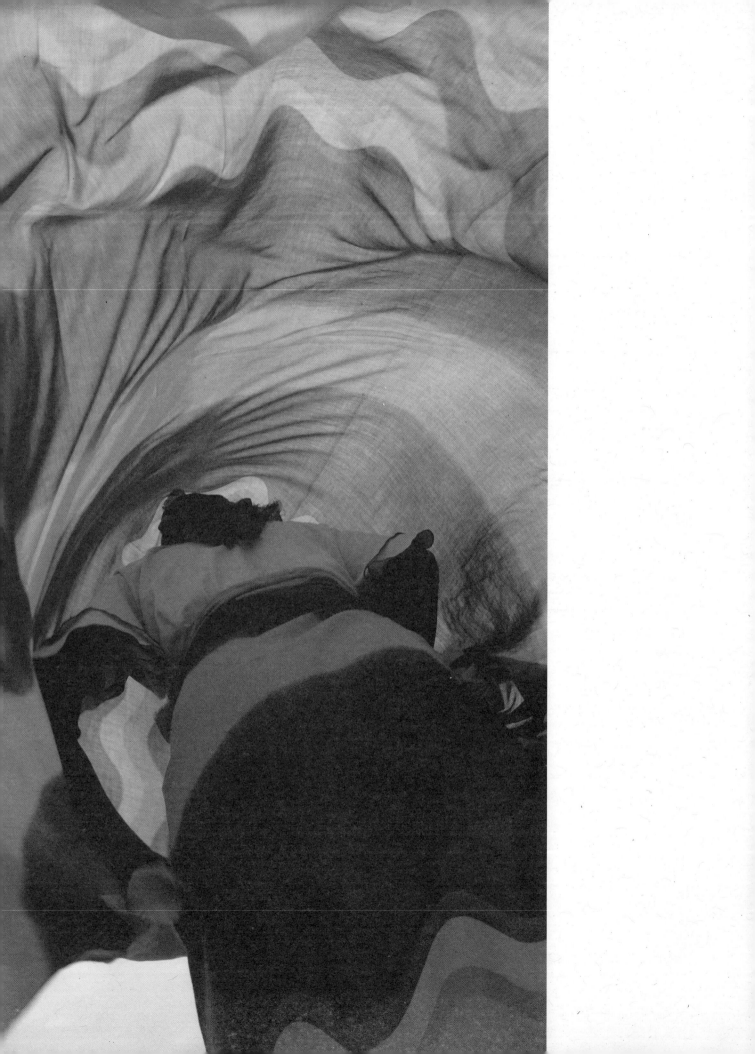

Chapter Five
The Church's Moral Authority and Sudan's Dream of Peace

The United Methodist Church, through its quadrennial General Conferences, has frequently spoken out on the matter of justice and peace in Sudan. United Methodists in Sudan and in the West can put legs on these formal churchwide directives through unified advocacy and prayer. Furthermore, we can join the global church in fostering the dream of peace. To start a flow of ideas, here are summaries or verbatim reports on General Conference actions, followed by a section on next steps for people of faith.

In 2004 the General Conference directed the General Boards of Global Ministries and Church and Society to monitor the "humanitarian crisis" in Sudan, to "work unceasingly" toward peace and reconciliation there, and to report back to the General Conference in 2008. The report read out to conference delegates meeting in Houston signaled United Methodist action on several fronts. Here is a summary.

How United Methodists Have Already Made a Difference

The General Boards of Global Ministries and Church and Society used on-the-ground observation and public policy forums to tell a compelling story of how United Methodists have combined their efforts to make a dramatic difference in the lives of countless people affected

by armed conflict not of their making. This action also demonstrates the strength of Christian love and hope in the face of bleak political and economic conditions.

In the area of relief and rehabilitation, much of the credit, though credit is not sought, for the on-site ministry goes to the Ginghamsburg United Methodist Church, near Tipp City, Ohio. This remarkable congregation was led by the Holy Spirit to step forward in faith to salvage the lives of thousands of displaced families and children.

The General Board of Church and Society did primary work in monitoring the international political and economic forces at work in Sudan and in keeping United Methodists informed on developments and positive responses they could make in the public policy arena. The board tracked the peace efforts of the United Nations and the Africa Union and made repeated attempts to influence both the UN and the United States government to take a creative role in seeking peace, justice, and reconciliation in the Darfur region. Tracking, education, and advocacy were also done by the Women's Division of Global Ministries.

Church and Society first addressed the situation in a formal way in October of 2004, in a resolution noting the "gravity of the atrocities committed against the local

A man in Dondona, an Arab village in South Darfur.

(Paul Jeffrey, ACT- Caritas)

population of Darfur." It urged the international community "to take all necessary steps to end the terror of civil conflict and the violence of hunger, disease, and displacement." A 2006 resolution made further specific proposals on peacekeeping measures and called for the disarming of the fighting groups.

The report went on to describe the partnership of United Methodist Committee on Relief and Ginghamsburg Church in South Darfur. Principles of their partnership included local purchasing to strengthen the economy in the region, providing incentives to nonfarm households to do the threshing, and providing agronomists, or agriculture experts, to show new technologies to the Darfur farmers, such as interplanting crops. Education and protection of children quickly became another priority of the partnership and soon expanded to include training to young adults in job skills such as masonry, carpentry, tailoring, and food processing. In 2007-08, the partners, together with other donors, were building 25 water stations in the region to serve some 250,000 people.

United Methodist Committee on Relief and its partners have had an opportunity to hear compelling voices in Southern Sudan and Darfur—the voices of children, heirs of a lost generation who can dream dreams. A visitor asked students in Southern Sudan what they want to be when they grow up. Some of their responses: doctor, nurse, teacher, president, pilot, lawyer, bishop, driver.

Resolution on Sudan: A Call to Compassion and Caring

As the General Conference of 2008 drew near, activists in the church wrote a resolution on Sudan to be considered by conference delegates. The resolution, accepted by the General Conference in its April-May sessions, calls for the prayerful engagement of United Methodists in nonviolent actions such as divestment (the release of church investment funds that support Sudan economic ventures); examining with care any actions of protest or solidarity before undertaking them; continuing to support humanitarian interventions through United Methodist Committee on Relief; and learning as much as possible about Sudan and its people. The resolution appears in full on the next pages.

Is not this the fast I choose: to loose the bonds of injustice, to undo the thongs of the yoke, to let the oppressed go free, and to break every yoke? Is it not to share your bread with the hungry, and bring the homeless poor into your house; when you see the naked, to cover them, and not to hide yourself from your own kin? Then your light shall break forth like the dawn, and your healing shall spring up quickly; your vindicator shall go before you, the glory of the Lord shall be your rear guard. (Isaiah 58:6-8)

Dr. Silvia Regina de Lima Silva, a Brazilian theologian, called for the walls to come down and the pathways to be opened towards a culture of compassion and caring. "… the words of Isaiah are directed towards those who have the power because they had the power to untie those who had been subjugated. On the other hand, the prophet also makes a call for solidarity among those who are tied to the same yoke. He invites them to change everyday relations, to seek forms of life in which bread can be eaten and shared, to live together, and to cover each other, and to protect and take care of each person's body. We understand this to be a call to compassion and caring."

"One million people have died since fighting began in our country in 1983. Three million people are now displaced. Yet there is nothing in your [Western] press about it. Are we not human beings?" These words were spoken in March 1989 by the Reverend Ezekiel Kutjok, General Secretary of the Sudan Council of Churches. In 2002 Church World Service in the United States expressed similar sentiments "Despite the enormous suffering and flagrant human rights abuses committed on all sides, the Sudan tragedy receives little attention from Western media. Churches and nongovernmental organizations have been at the forefront of efforts to respond to the suffering of Sudan's peoples and support their creative efforts

to build a just and lasting peace." That is the solidarity which Isaiah calls for with the people of Sudan as they painstakingly rebuild their country, changing everyday relations, and finding ways of sharing with each other.

That same year Church World Service emphasized that the Sudan was as a country "Hungry for Peace," saying that "the Sudan suffers from the world's longest running civil war—35 of the last 46 years. Fueled by religious, ethnic, and political differences between the country's Northern and Southern populations, more than two million Sudanese, mostly in the South, have died as a result of this conflict. Three hundred Sudanese die each day from war-related causes. More than 4.5 million people are internally displaced, and over 500,000 have fled to other countries as refugees." In this civil war the colonial past and the growing economic concerns were also crucial to understanding the roots of the conflict. They included, among others, the sequels of serious drought and famine in Northern and Western Sudan in 1984-85 and in the South in 1986-88; conflicts between pastoralists and agriculturalists; and the vast resources of oil in the South.

The World Council of Churches helped broker a peace accord between North and South which lasted 11 years—the country's only peaceful period since independence from joint Egyptian-British rule in 1956. In 2002 the WCC appointed a special ecumenical envoy, the Rev. Dr. Samuel Kobia (the organization's current General Secretary) to accompany the peace negotiations between the government of the Sudan/National Congress Party in Northern Sudan and the Sudan People's Liberation Movement (SPLM) in Southern Sudan. Their Comprehensive Peace Agreement (CPA) was finalized January 2005. The agreement included a permanent cease fire and autonomy for Southern Sudan for 6 years with a referendum about independence to be held in 2011. An autonomous government was formed in the

South and a power-sharing government was set up in Khartoum with the South represented by a co-vice president. It was further agreed that North and South would share equally in the oil revenues. The United Nations was authorized to support the CPA and a peacekeeping operation was sent including 10,000 troops and 600 police. International donors pledged $4.5 billion in aid to recover from the decades of war.

The Republic of Sudan is the largest country in Africa. Situated in the Greater Horn of Africa, it is surrounded by Egypt to the North and moving clockwise, the Red Sea, Eritrea, Ethiopia, Kenya, Uganda, Democratic Republic of the Congo, Central African Republic, Chad, and Libya. The Sudan was one of the most ethnically and linguistically diverse countries in the world. "In 1999 it had nearly 600 ethnic groups speaking over 400 languages and dialects. During the 80s and 90s smaller ethnic and linguistic groups disappeared. Migration played a part, as migrants often forget their native tongue when they move to an area dominated by another language. Some linguistic groups were absorbed by accommodation, others by conflict." Arabic is the official language but English and many languages and dialects are spoken in the Sudan. The Sudanese population is approximately 37 million people: 70 percent Sunni Muslim; 25 percent have indigenous beliefs; and 5 percent are Christians.

While the Comprehensive Peace Agreement was being negotiated, violent conflict broke out in the Western states. In February 2003 world attention was directed to Darfur (the land of the Fur people). There are several other ethnic groups in Darfur. A rebellion began, initiating a number of military activities leading to a grave humanitarian situation. In April 2003 coordinated attacks against military targets in the regional capital of Al Fasher were launched by the Sudan Liberation Movement (SLA) and the Justice and Equality Movement (JEM).The Sudan government responded harshly as it had during the conflict with the South, using counterinsurgency tactics and indiscriminate aerial bombings. Its armed forces coordinated with irregular militia (including *janjaweed*, or men on horseback, known for raping women, pillaging, and looting the population in Darfur) to attack not only the rebel forces but the civilian populations causing thousands to die, vast destruction by burning down whole villages, trees and fields, and the displacement of hundreds of thousands of people. Rebel groups were also involved in the disastrous consequences of their armed attacks against the government.

Violence in Darfur escalated rapidly leading to more than 200,000 deaths caused by killings, illness, and starvation due to the scorched-earth policy; 2.1 million internally displaced persons; and 236,000 as refugees in Chad. The situation became known as one of the worst humanitarian disasters in the 21st century. The cruelty of the armed attacks on the civilian population was reminiscent of the same in South Sudan and in the neighboring Democratic Republic of the Congo where it is estimated that 4 million people died. Women and children were particularly vulnerable to sexual abuse. The age-old struggle for land suggested that attackers, especially the *janjaweed*, were killing and burning down homes to move people away and replace them. A rebellion against the government in Khartoum became an opportunity to revive old rivalries, settle scores, and take over the farmlands for grazing cattle.

Solidarity with the people of Sudan raised an outcry around the world demanding an end to the massacres, the atrocities, and bringing the perpetrators to justice for crimes against humanity and, as some nongovernmental organizations suggested, ethnic cleansing. In the United States, officials and legislators, churches and nongovernmental organizations accused the Sudan of genocide.

The United Nations sent a team to investigate but in their report they noted that there were crimes against humanity but not enough evidence that the government of the Sudan had "intent to destroy…" The Convention on the Prevention and Punishment of the Crime of Genocide does define genocide as any act "committed with intent to destroy, in whole or in part, a national, ethnical, racial, or religious group…" The protest against the Sudan promoted many demonstrations, vigils, visits to Darfur, and eventually a divestment movement which promoted international sanctions which the Security Council discussed but never agreed to.

The Sudan government, the militias, the rebel movement, and neighboring governments as the conflict spilled over their borders were among those with influence or power to end the conflict. Other actors included the United Nations Security Council and the African Union, headquartered in Addis Ababa, which responded with help in containing the chaos by sending in monitors, peacekeepers, and police.

The Security Council was sending peacekeeping forces and police to the South of Sudan. The Council was already responsible for 18 peacekeeping operations on four continents involving 100,000 personnel, directly impacting the lives of hundreds of millions of people. Yet, the African forces needed reinforcement and support and the Council began to discuss how they could raise another peacekeeping mission. Other involved powers were the five permanent members in the Security Council—the United Kingdom, China, France, Russia, and the United States. Each of these have political and strategic interests, as well as economic stakes, in the Sudan, which is rich with resources such as oil, natural gas, uranium, gold, silver, chrome, manganese, and other minerals.

Finally, all those in power or with influence, including the worldwide protesters against continued violence and those in the solidarity movement with the Sudanese people, were able to agree on common solutions symbolized by the renewed peace talks between the Sudanese government, the rebel groups and militias and the unanimous approval in the Security Council to authorize the "hybrid UN-African Union operation in Darfur." In the United Nations press release of July 31, 2007, the Security Council approved the creation of a hybrid United Nations-African Union peacekeeping force to quell the violence and instability plaguing the Darfur region of Sudan. In what Secretary-General Ban Ki-moon called a "historic and unprecedented resolution," council members unanimously backed the establishment of a force of nearly 20,000 military personnel and more than 6,000 police officers.

Decades of negligence and marginalization by both the former colonial powers and the Sudanese government were major causes for the rebellion. "Over the course of the 20th century, colonial and independence governments in Khartoum (the capital of Sudan) devoted few resources to developing the human potential of Darfur. There were limited investments in infrastructure, schooling, and economic activity." In addition, since most residents were either involved with raising livestock or in low-productivity agriculture, recent droughts and the advancing desert exacerbated tensions over access to water and fertile land, crucial causes for the rebellion. Fredrick Nzwili, a freelance journalist from Kenya writing for the Ecumenical Water Network, agrees. "From Darfur in western Sudan to Mt. Elgon in Kenya, the absence of water for rural communities is emerging as a major cause of conflict on the African continent. In Darfur, the story is one of pain and desperation for the nearly two million displaced persons. And the organizations that work in the area are convinced that it is battles for water and pasture that sparked it off."

The United Nations Environment Program (UNEP) released a report in June 2007 saying, "indeed historical data in Darfur indicates that rainfall declines of between 16 percent and over 30 percent have occurred turning millions of hectares of marginal semi-desert land into desert...Overall, deserts in some northern regions of Sudan may have advanced by an average of 100 km over the past 40 years....The scale of climate change recorded in Northern Darfur is almost unprecedented, and its impacts are closely linked to the conflicts in the region, as desertification has added significantly to the stress on traditional agricultural and pastoral livelihoods...the crisis is being aggravated by degradation of water sources in deserts known as wadis or oases. 'Virtually all such areas inspected by UNEP were found to be moderately to severely degraded, principally due to deforestation, overgrazing, and erosion.'"

United Methodists praise God for signs of hope. As in the Social Principles (*The Book of Discipline of The United Methodist Church, 2004*, ¶165B,) we can applaud worldwide efforts to develop more just international economic systems in which the limited resources of the earth will be used to the maximum benefit of all nations and peoples. Another sign of hope is the ability of UMCOR to work in Southern Darfur, an area which its assessment team determined was underserved by other agencies. UMCOR'S programs in Southern Darfur assist hundreds of thousands of people, including providing seeds and tools to farmers, schools and supplies to children, training for teachers, vocational training programs, and establishing water points. Ten water points have been completed, giving some 250,000 Sudanese access to water. In 2006, UMCOR began working in South Sudan to assist the people returning home after nearly 20 years of war.

As Dr. Lima Silva says, solidarity means finding ways "to seek forms of life in which bread can be eaten and shared to live together, and to cover each other, and to protect and take care of each person's body." For United Methodists this is a call to compassion and caring.

Therefore:

1. The United Methodist Church should affirm and call upon all parties to work through and with the United Nations and the African Union to secure justice for all Sudanese.
2. United Methodists in every country should encourage their governments and the economic entities within their societies to aid and work for the development of a more just economic system in the Sudan.
3. United Methodists should examine all methods of protest and solidarity before undertaking them. Recent efforts by the divestment movement in the United States, in which many United Methodists participated, is an example of a nonviolent strategy to effect change and has contributed to raising awareness of the plight of the people in Darfur. As United Methodists continue to seek a just and lasting peace in Sudan, we should ensure that none of their actions cause violence.
4. United Methodists should commend the General Board of Global Ministries for its development of a mission study on the Sudan and should take advantage of all opportunities to study and develop a better understanding of all the people in the Sudan.
5. United Methodists should continue to contribute to UMCOR and commend them for their ongoing work in the Sudan, remembering that the 2004 General Conference commended them for their concern and caring for Darfur refugees in Chad.

Call for Divestment "Pull money out"

As US president, George W. Bush signed into law legislation allowing state and local governments to cut their investment ties to Sudan. A few months later the General Conference in 2008 also approved a petition for divestment of business interests and investments in companies who do business in Sudan. Thus United Methodists joined a growing group of organizations calling for divestment, including the NAACP, which termed divestment "a proven tool in struggles against inhumane governments. Americans' divestment was a major contributor to bringing down the racist apartheid regime in South Africa in the 1980s," said the NAACP, "when people, municipalities (including the federal government), and corporations pulled billions of dollars out of that country rather than make money off of an immoral government that supported slavery."

International Criminal Court Role

The church can urge Sudan and Southern Sudan to create a culture of accountability as part of achieving the dream of peace in the region. In February 2007 the chief prosecutor of the International Criminal Court, Luis Moreno-Ocampo, took a step that among some Dafurians was regarded as small but crucial progress in securing a sustainable end to the violence in Darfur. Moreno-Ocampo named names—two individuals suspected of committing some of the worst atrocities in Darfur. Both men are connected with the Khartoum government. One is a junior-level executive in the government, the first government official ever cited by the International Criminal Court; one is a member of the so-called *janjaweed*, the paramilitary group that may receive some of its support and armaments from the Khartoum government.

Writing for *The Nation*, Darfur native Salih Mahmoud Osman said, "This alone is a profound step forward for those of us who struggle every day to put an end to the worst crimes imaginable." But, he went on to write, it isn't enough. He calls for a "sequence of cases," and for higher aim.

Higher aim became a reality in July 2008 when the court's chief prosecutor asked a panel of three judges to issue an arrest warrant for Sudan's president, Omar al-Bashir, for genocide and crimes against humanity, including murder, torture, and rape. At a news conference at The Hague, Luis Moreno-Ocampo told reporters, "al-Bashir organized the destitution, insecurity, and harassment of the survivors [of a failed counterinsurgency]. He did not need bullets. He used other weapons: rapes, hunger, and fear. As efficient, but silent." The judges were expected to take several months to sort through the evidence presented by the prosecutor. The short-term effect of this action was mixed—some Sudanese rallied around their leader, while European Union and United Nations officials expressed fears that there could be reprisals against aid workers and peacekeepers in Darfur and a backlash against the peace process. The government of Sudan does not recognize the authority of the court.

United Methodists have stated support for the activities of the court. A resolution presented to the 2008 General Conference said in part:

"The United Methodist Church calls on the Council of Bishops, all agencies, commissions, local churches, districts, annual and central conferences to witness to the urgent need to stop the destruction of life and to seek resources, develop resources, and share resources, in as many languages as possible and through the varied means available in The United Methodist Church. Such resources should enable members of The United Methodist Church to:

a. Remain informed and work towards the prevention of conflicts, atrocities, violence, and suffering which is borne by millions of people in the world.

b. Participate in the World Council of Churches' mobilization of the churches for peace and join other organizations and movements which struggle for peace with justice.

c. Assure the presence and participation of the church in those places where people need protection and humanitarian aid.

d. Remain informed on the work of the International Criminal Court and become supportive of the court's work.

e. Support organizations working for human rights and be watchful and critical of the new Human Rights Council of the United Nations as it develops its new structures and procedures.

The statement also encouraged local churches to assist in capacity development, create public-private partnerships that can strengthen civil society, and "offer their moral authority" in mediating meaningful agreements between conflicting sides.

Sustainability of Peace

Other diplomats and those concerned with global justice have proposed additional steps. Here are some of them:

- Work for a more comprehensive approach to the peace process, including increased roles for women and a focus on local conflict resolution.

- Insist on unconditional access by humanitarian agencies to survivors, displaced persons, and women and children who have experienced sexual violence since the start.

- Pressure the Khartoum government to cease military flights and to end its support of complicit militias.

- Reconstitute a permanent ceasefire commission and empower it to conduct negotiations among all the parties.

- Urge neighboring states, such as Chad and Cameroon and Libya, Central African Republic, and Uganda, to commit to a genuine peace process that stops the flow of arms between opposition groups operating out of those nations and Sudan opposition groups.

These recommendations may help to stabilize the present conditions and create an environment where additional work could be done. For the long term, the economic justice issues must also be addressed.

Major initiatives are needed to dismantle the war economy that favors some elites over the majority; to build up the weak infrastructure, providing health care and good water and schooling; and, perhaps most importantly, to redirect the grab from the outside for control of resources away from economic powerhouses like China and the United States and back toward the people of Sudan. They should have a right to determine where and how the riches of their country should be harvested and spent to serve their needs.

The funding for such initiatives can come in part from humanitarian aid agencies like UMCOR. But the scale of the needed construction requires large infusions of money and workers, well beyond the capability of private charity to provide in Sudan. As Uzodinma Iweala

Women celebrate the everyday joys despite living in a camp for internally displaced people outside the village of Kubum, in Sudan's West Darfur state.

(Paul Jeffrey, ACT- Caritas)

wrote in his 2007 *Washington Post* essay, Sudan could use international partners—partners who make a commitment not only to build pipelines and pump oil away from the country, but to also build roads, water systems, access to electricity or solar power, decent housing, schools, hospitals, and community centers.

Manuel Aranda da Silva, the United Nations' humanitarian coordinator in Khartoum, told a delegation of United Methodists and UMCOR staff in August 2005 that replacing lost infrastructure would be a "seven-day-a-week, fifteen-hour-a-day job." The need to transform the community into a culture of peace will take not just reconstruction, da Silva emphasized, but construction from scratch. The years of war have left virtually nothing in place.

How Sudanese Women Are Modeling Peace

To put it bluntly, peace and justice in Sudan (and in all other countries that deliberately marginalize women) will be only a dream until women take their rightful place as leaders. With terrible abuses layering over all

the other woes such as displacement and poverty, how can the leadership of women be encouraged? And, in light of the mandate of global diplomats to include women in the process, how shall women lead in Sudan? The United Methodist Church and United Methodist Women can advocate for women's leadership at all levels of the peace process.

The good news is, Sudanese women are already modeling peacebuilding in their communities. One way is through education. Jane Ohuma, UMCOR's inaugural head of mission in Sudan, said, "Educate a woman; educate all Sudan." This is a common saying throughout the continent. Education—especially the education of girls and women—is a priority in achieving a sustainable peace.

Early Christian missionaries from Great Britain pioneered girls' schools. But on the whole, only about half the women in Sudan over the age of 15 can read and write. Sudan has developed as a solidly traditional, patriarchal culture. Even the lives of women are less valuable than those of men. John Bul Dau reports that in his village in Duk County, Southern Sudan, if a woman died in an accident her family would be compensated about half the number of cattle as if a man had died—though "both had great value."

So in Sudan, as in many parts of Africa, these circumstances make it difficult to identify women's leadership—especially with Western definitions of the term. Indeed, this is the dilemma for women in any patriarchal society, but it is especially the dilemma in Africa and in Sudan. Leadership as understood and practiced by many Western women—that is, the ability to be outspoken, conduct business on an equal footing with men, have innate authority, command respect for one's opinions, expect to be heard, hold high office or positions in secular and church structures, and so on—and leadership as understood and practiced by women in Sudan may not look the same at all. Mary Modupe Kolawole puts our potential dissonance into a perspective with four points about the way she understands African (and Sudanese) women to exercise their leadership now.

- Women are leaders in the family. Kolawole says women "carry the burden" of the family's economic survival.

- Women are leaders in creating self-esteem for themselves from the debasements of colonialism by giving voice to their own unique experiences as African women.

- Women are leaders in cherishing their roles as mothers or potential mothers because that role is so crucial to the formation and preservation of indigenous social, moral, and cultural values, including the fine arts and performing arts.

For example in Sudan specifically, Kolawole writes, the arts play a role unique to Nuba grandmothers, whose storytelling is a cultural institution. In Northern Sudan the form of folk poetry known as *hija* satirizes people's moral laxity and is used almost exclusively by women for self-expression.

- Fourth, women are leaders in reinventing traditional stories, poetry, songs, and other oral masterpieces to reframe women as sources of virtue and to strengthen the image of women.

Baqie Badawi Muhammad enlarges our understanding of women's leadership in Darfur specifically through her explanation of a socio-political institution of *al-Hakkama*, in which women enjoy the powerful right to criticize or compliment anyone—including the chief. Such a critical feminine voice comes from the self-awareness and social emancipation that categorizes women as socially and politically active. Muhammad collected songs during her 1994 fieldwork in West Darfur that explicitly commented on the political situation in Sudan, including the rising prices of commodities and the policies of international actors like the International Monetary Fund. "While women singers are not decision makers at the governmental level, through their songs they…urge people to take responsibility for their own freedom," wrote Muhammad. She pointed out that according to Islamic doctrine, "Woman was not created in order to remain within the household's sphere, never to emerge." In fact, she wrote, one of the women of the family of Prophet Muhammad (Peace Be Upon Him), Khadija, was a businesswoman in long distance trade.

From observations during her fieldwork, wrote Muhammad, Darfurian women "take on both domestic and production roles, working inside and outside the home, distinguishing themselves from other Muslim women in

Sudan." She wrote that women of Darfur work as butchers and construction workers. As noted in an UMCOR field visit in 2005, women were working as farmers. In Khartoum some women work in the government offices as assistants or secretaries. And of course in rural Sudan women work very hard. They must carry water, collect firewood, prepare meals, and care for the young children. Food production and preservation were among the many modes of creativity that Darfurian women used to develop and maintain a means of endurance.

At a conference of the Sudan Studies Association held in May 2008 other perspectives suggested important roles for Sudanese women in the peace process and future development of their country. Ten Sudanese political activists expressed the consensus of all the papers addressing women's participation in Sudan when they told researcher Margaret Otto of the University of Berlin that sustainable peace efforts in Sudan will require the participation of everyone in the country—women in particular. These women saw that statement in stark contrast to the traditional constraints of family law and the far-reaching control that men have over life in general. Yet the women hold up forgiveness and social justice as critical to reconciliation and long-term peace.

The United Nations Security Council Resolution #1325, "Women, Peace and Security," mandated that women participate in the peace process. According to the research of Sacha Chambers of Nova Southeastern University, Sudanese women "have been consistently sidelined"—yet they have still made their mark. Some events have been held in Darfur, for instance, by UN groups, the World Bank, and the US Department of State, where women could discuss strategies for peace. Women have tried creative approaches too, sowing the seeds of dialogue and unity among their own communities. In Darfur artists responded to the conflict by creating new patterns in basketry as a coping strategy, and also as a way to document the horror of famine and other social events. Some women in Southern Sudan told their stories in a film, "Acts of Love: The Struggle for Sudan," their words conveying the people's hope and love for the land.

The people not only love their land and hold hope for Sudan, but they are exhibiting leadership by maintaining a life of dignity. To illustrate an example of this kind of leadership Baqie Badawi Muhammad told the story of seventy-year-old Haja Nasra. When the government in her Darfur town confiscated her donkey to use in a security detail, she was "fearless, aggressive, and a powerful fighter," wrote Muhammad, who witnessed Haja Nasra's confrontation of the town Sheikh, or judge. Like the woman of Jesus' parable who argued for justice until the judge gave in "so she may not wear me out," Haja Nasra prevailed. She presented herself as a woman whose donkey was the only means by which she could provide water to her large family. The Sheikh restored her donkey.

How the Global Church Is Fostering Peace in Sudan

Noting that "the fate of the people of Sudan seems to oscillate between hope and despair," the World Council of Churches urged the ecumenical community to "undertake advocacy and lobby work for the implementation of the agreements [in the Comprehensive Peace Agreement], make fact-finding and solidarity visits to the region, and provide the much-needed humanitarian assistance and support." In her more than 20 years of advocacy work for Sudan, Marina Peter, European coordinator of the Sudan Ecumenical Forum, cautioned that "any contribution to a better future for the people needs to be based on an understanding of the complexity and interdependence of the country." She encouraged churches in Sudan to play a watchdog role, "challenging the government when it does something wrong, because people in Sudan, including many Muslims, listen to the churches."

Reviving the Failed State

Sudan's churches could advocate for leaders who put the people first—in the North, the South, and the so-called transitional zones in the East, such as the Nuba and Southern Blue Nile people. Much has been made of the strategies of divestment, economic sanctions, and other pressures on the government of Sudan to bring about peace. The United Methodist Church has, as explained above, joined others in these strategies to bring pressure. The potential benefits of such economic punishments are wrapped-up in their ability to sway a government to see that a change in approach is tantamount to acting in its own interest.

Contrarily, these measures could have the disastrous effect of collapse of the central government. Such collapses, like that in Somalia in the 1990s, do not bode well. In Somalia the failure of government led to clan- and tribe-driven wars from which Somalia has not yet been able to recover.

Though it is very difficult for outsiders to create any meaningful structure for recovery of Sudan and Southern Sudan, the United Nations High Commissioner for Human Rights offered five recommendations to assist Sudan in meeting its international and domestic human rights obligations. The summary below is adapted from "Second Periodic Report of the UNHCHR" published in 2005.

1. Implementing a Culture of Accountability

In areas where peace has taken hold in Sudan, the government should focus on ending the "culture of impunity" and open the way to a new "culture of accountability."

The judiciary must be adequately financed, reformed, and staffed with professionals. Immunity laws for state agents, regardless of their official status, should be revoked. This is particularly true for personnel with powers of arrest and detention. Law enforcement and military forces in all states and in the transitional areas should be held accountable for their actions. The government should cease its attacks on civilians, disarm militias, and install an active, professional, well-trained law enforcement system with adequate resources.

Persons who have not yet been held accountable for the commission of prior crimes, including those relating to the 21-year civil war, should be brought to justice. The Comprehensive Peace Agreement calls for a reconciliation process, and this should be one of its key components. The government must also put the weight of action and political will behind its numerous commitments to accountability, so far unrealized.

2. National Security Reform

The interim constitution created with the Comprehensive Peace Agreement, envisioned reform of the national security organizations that were acting with abusive and unchecked powers of arrest and detention. This relates to the calls of removing immunity protections in domestic law.

3. Respecting Economic, Social, and Cultural Rights

Conflict in Sudan was initially sparked in response to practices of marginalization and discriminatory resource allocation. The wars that followed resulted in further devastation to health, education, and living conditions. To remedy this, resource allocation must be fair, transparent, nondiscriminatory, and inclusive of the affected communities. The government should partner with humanitarian and development agencies, particularly where it may be unable to provide the required services itself.

4. A Free Civil Society

The government must allow civil society to function freely. Restrictions on the creation and activities of media outlets and associations, including political parties and unions, should be the exception rather than the rule.

5. Effective Use of the National Law Reform Committee

In 2005 the Ministry of Justice established a committee for law reform. Its mandate was to review the compatibility of legislation adopted over the past 100 years, culminating in the interim constitution. This process should result in the harmonization of Sudan's domestic legislation with its obligations under international human rights law. In addition the committee should strengthen nondiscrimination laws and laws pertaining to the rights of women.

"Painting Things Awake": What Next for Sudan?

Being in Darfur and seeing Khartoum and Southern Sudan are humbling experiences. The situation there on so many fronts resists achieving the truth. The situation is complicated—horribly so. Heartbreakingly, horrible violence has occurred. Systematic rape has been a war strategy. It appears that if not killing on a genocidal scale, at least ethnic cleansing has been a strategy as well. Yet the people persist. This is apparent in the community of Sudanese artists, writers, and poets who continue to produce their art and poetry in spite of persecution. One of them, Al-Saddiq Al-Raddi, used the term "painting things awake" to suggest how his people are not only enduring but prevailing. How may we, as people of faith, help to paint things awake in Sudan from our long distance? Here are some possible next steps.

Certainly all who study Sudan and its plight agree there must be accountability. People who perpetrated these crimes against humanity must be brought to justice. It is also important that African systems of justice, like the Truth and Reconciliation Commission model developed in South Africa, be examined for relevance and invoked or reinvented to fit the situation in Sudan.

Did the truth and reconciliation process deliver for South Africa? And would a similar process deliver for Sudan? The South African process went beyond truth-seeking in its broader mandate to foster national unity. If this were to be designed for Sudan, the Sudanese selected for truth commissions would have to be above reproach. All sides in the complex mix would have to be represented, not just the "victors," whoever they may be. A study conducted by researchers in the psychiatric department of the University of Stellenbosch, Tygerberg, South Africa, concluded that a truth and reconciliation process should form a part of a process of reintegration and unity within a nation torn as Sudan has been, but not be relied on as the only approach taken toward peace and reconciliation.

To its credit the government of Sudan was acknowledging at this writing that a process like the Truth and Reconciliation Commission might be important for the nation's long-term health. Professor Ahmad E. Elbashir, a former professor at the University of the District of Columbia in the United States and at this writing a staff member in the Ministry of Foreign Affairs of the government of Sudan (he is part of the Council of International People's Friendship) told an interfaith delegation that "the model for reconciliation in Darfur must be grounded in indigenous community and tribal

A girl arrives at school in the morning in the Dereig Camp for internally displaced persons.

(Paul Jeffrey, ACT- Caritas)

A boy living in the Kubum Camp for internally displaced persons.

(Paul Jeffrey, ACT- Caritas)

relationship models." A spirit of discernment must be part of the approach. Professor Elbashir, a native of Sudan, taught at the University of the District Columbia and published a book about slavery in the Horn of Africa before his employment with the government. Professor Elbashir's other talking points were closely allied with the government of Sudan's positions. However, the church might find much to agree with in the list. They included:

• Seek dialogue.

• Express the call by the interfaith community for an end to all forms of armed conflict and human rights violations in Sudan. (Such calls have been issued not only by faith-based groups but also by United Nations agencies, humanitarian agencies, and the international community.)

• All allegations of human rights abuses, rape, and genocide must be fully investigated. (Investigations have been conducted, to little effect on the government of Sudan, so far. The findings of the International Criminal Court in July 2008, the first call for the

arrest of a sitting leader for crimes against humanity and genocide, may have a more profound effect.)

• In consultation with all the parties to the conflict in Sudan, discern how members of the Abrahamic faith communities might play a meaningful role in providing humanitarian relief to people suffering from the effects of war and poverty. Interfaith cooperation is already affecting resettlement of internally displaced persons and land mine removal in war-affected areas of Southern Sudan.

• Recognize the centrality of women to a sustainable peace process, and the role that women today play in all dimensions of national leadership in Sudan.

• Normalize relations between the United States and Sudan's governments through withdrawal of economic sanctions.

• Recognize that the problems of Darfur and peace in between the North and South must be solved by the people of Sudan themselves.

But Omer Ismail cautions: "Peace will not come to [Sudan] in isolation." He means that the government-friendly view (solutions from the people of Sudan) is not likely to have much impact in the long run. Ismail, a native of Darfur, is a contributor to "Sudan Peace and Democracy Watch," a website of the Center for American Progress, an organization that since 2007 has advocated for international intervention in Sudan. Whether international intervention is successful or whether Sudanese people themselves can bring peace and justice through concerted action of their own, one learns quickly in Sudan to avoid making claims. Here no single entity is in control. It is too big; there are too many issues, too many competing entities and agendas.

Mission Study Ends, But the Dream of Peace Goes On

This mission study resource on Sudan ends here, but the story of Sudan and its dream of peace and justice have not yet found their resolution. Sudan still bleeds. Its afflictions go on, but out of the limelight. In 2008 world leaders and media were consumed with other stories: a devastating earthquake in China's province of Sechuan; a cyclone in Myanmar that killed and displaced tens of thousands; a brief but lethal war in the Republic of Georgia; the summer Olympics, coincidentally being staged by Sudan's great trading partner, China. Sudan and its troubles seemed so far away. With few exceptions they were off camera, absent from the top stories of the day. In previous years Sudan competed with other news—for instance, the South Asia tsunami and Hurricane Katrina. Yet Sudan still bleeds, on or off the front page.

Our faith assures us that God has not abandoned the people of Sudan. And, a culture that has survived and thrived for so many centuries through so much warfare has steel in it. The Sudanese poet Al-Saddiq Al-Raddi, who has been jailed by the current government for his activism and his lyric poetry, suggests metaphorically how the stirrings of liberty, leadership, and peace stay alive in Sudan. His poem, "A Monkey at the Window," uses the symbol of a small, playful child, to affirm that the spirit of the Sudanese is strong. He affirms the faith that the people of Sudan will "paint things awake"—will transcend their varied and conflicting tribal heritages, the oppression of colonial times, and today's crushing issues, to realize the birth of a strong, viable nation.

The solid front door remembers the hand that
made it.
You are the key —
and the creak of the universe—it's your sole
secret.
You lean your dreams and future against it.
For its sake you endure the woodworms
gnawing through your heart,
the reek of damp,
the hammering of enemies and relatives.
(Long is the absence of light
that paints things awake —
Long is the presence of paint.)

Al-Raddi himself might punctuate this vision with the Muslim benediction "Insha'Allah," meaning "if God wills it." To move to a civil society with an infrastructure that ensures the good life for all its citizens, empowers democratically elected leaders, encourages freedom from want and freedom to worship, and sustains peace and justice for all is a process that took Europeans and Americans many centuries. Even so, in some places that work is still not complete. Like other countries in Africa, Sudan does not have centuries. People of faith everywhere can humbly offer prayers of support and love in this critical time. Let us resolve, so far as it depends on us, to do what we can to paint things awake; to advocate the hard path of peace and justice for the people of Sudan.

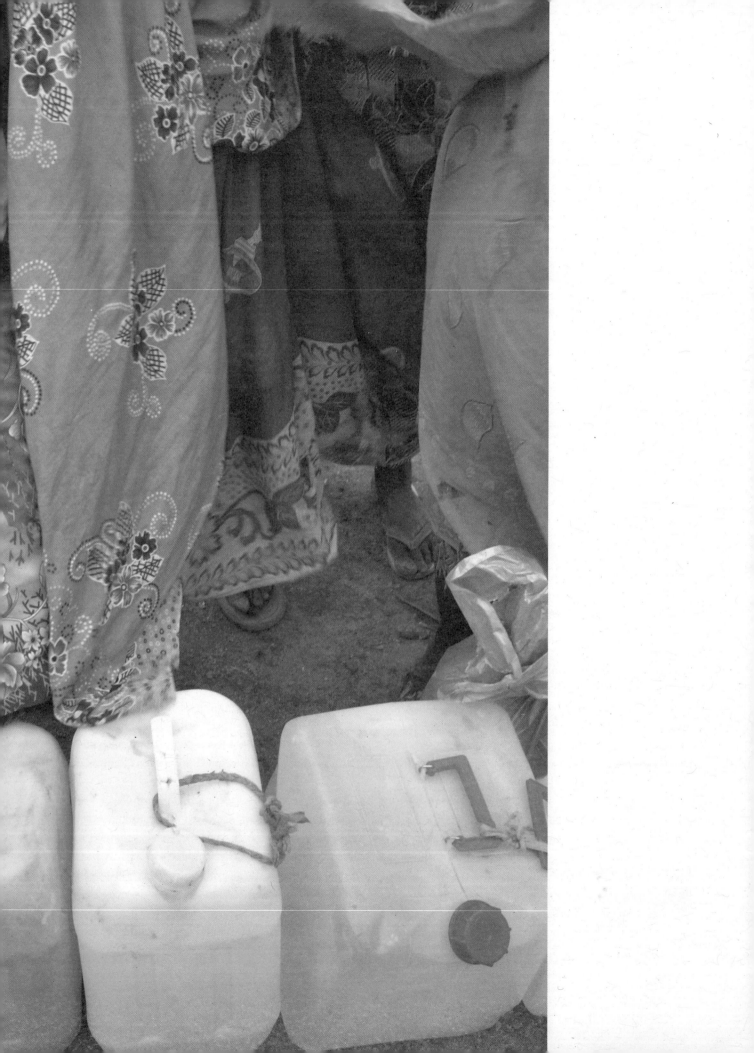

Glossary

Berkeb—Yogurt preserved by Darfurian women.

Dinar—Sudanese currency, replaced in 2007 with the new Sudanese pound. Each dinar earned by Saba, the woman in Chapter Two living in a Khartoum displaced persons camp in 2005, was equivalent to less than one cent in US currency.

Drover—A herder of animals.

Ema—Man's headcovering.

Gotia (also spelled qutiyya)—Conical-shaped shelters with straight side walls made from mud and thatch.

Hijab—Headscarf worn by Muslim women; used to refer to modest dress.

Insha'Allah—A benediction meaning "If God wills it," found as a directive in the Holy Qur'an (Surah Al-Kahf, 18:23-24).

Lorry—British term for a truck commonly used in Sudan to identify open-bed vehicles.

Malwah—Measure for grain, enough to plant 16 hectares.

Markoub—Slippers similar to mules, often made of goatskin, worn by men.

Mu'adhdhin—The man who chants the *azan*, or call to prayer, from the mosque.

Niqab—Veil worn by Muslim women.

Omda—Leader in a community who reports in to the headman, or sheikh.

Polygyny—The practice of marriage to more than one woman at a time. This contrasts with polygamy, marriage in which a spouse of either sex has more than one mate at a time.

Rakouba—Open-sided pole building with roofing made of woven grasses.

Ramadan—Monthlong spiritual fast between sunrise and sunset, observed annually by Muslims.

Souk—Arabic word meaning marketplace.

Sheikh—Headman or community leader; judge.

Taub—Length of cloth worn as a traditional wrap by many Sudanese women.

Timeline

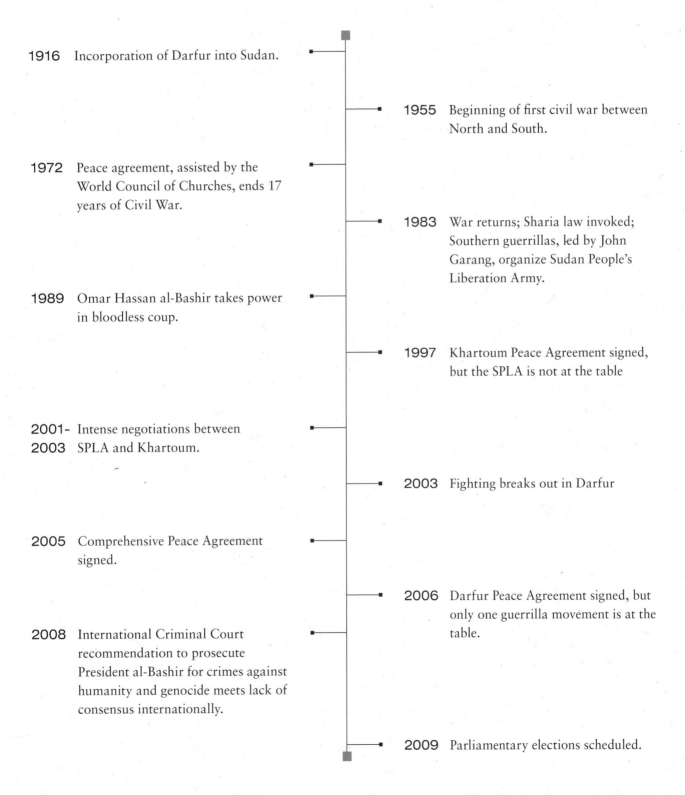

1916   Incorporation of Darfur into Sudan.

1955   Beginning of first civil war between North and South.

1972   Peace agreement, assisted by the World Council of Churches, ends 17 years of Civil War.

1983   War returns; Sharia law invoked; Southern guerrillas, led by John Garang, organize Sudan People's Liberation Army.

1989   Omar Hassan al-Bashir takes power in bloodless coup.

1997   Khartoum Peace Agreement signed, but the SPLA is not at the table

2001-   Intense negotiations between
2003   SPLA and Khartoum.

2003   Fighting breaks out in Darfur

2005   Comprehensive Peace Agreement signed.

2006   Darfur Peace Agreement signed, but only one guerrilla movement is at the table.

2008   International Criminal Court recommendation to prosecute President al-Bashir for crimes against humanity and genocide meets lack of consensus internationally.

2009   Parliamentary elections scheduled.

Notes

Sources are given for direct quotations, identified by a key phrase from the quote, for most numbers and statistics, and for many other points of information. When facts involved are not in dispute or can easily be found in one or more key books or articles, sources are omitted. The writer is especially indebted to Sudan scholars Baqie Badawi Muhammad, Alex de Waal, and Gerard Prunier; to womanist scholars Mary E. Modupe Kolawole and Ife Amadiume; and to Adam Hochschild, whose chilling and heartbreaking accounts of colonialists' treatment of people of the Congo woke her up.

Introduction

3   More than anything: Kapuscinski, 3.
5   City populations in Sudan: Brinkhoff, City Population.
5-6   Rumbek: Fisher in BBC news release, January 21, 2005.
6   "There is still a lot that the West needs to know": Kolawole, 20.
8   "Enactment of a no-fly zone": Rieff, *Los Angeles Times*, June 24, 2007.
8   Outworn ideas about native people. An excellent discussion of the impact of European colonial attitudes and actions may be found in Hochschild, 61-74.
9   "Loving eye": McFague, 32.

Chapter One: A Sense of Place

11   "Lake the size of Lake Erie": Polgreen, *The New York Times*, July 22, 2007.
11   Exports: *CIA Factbook*, May 2008.
11-12   Sociological contrasts: *Encyclopedia Britannica Online*, "The Sudan."
12   "Arabized Sudanese": Prunier, 77; Flint and de Waal, 15.
12   Median age: *CIA Factbook*, May 2008.
12-15   Historical perspective: *Encyclopedia Britannica Online* and *Wikipedia*; also de Waal, Prunier.
15   Sidebar material: *CIA Factbook*, May 2008.
16   Treaty with Libya: Prunier, 69.
16   Sudan and the US on information: Prunier, 89.
16   Facilitation of peace process: The Sudan Experience Interview Questions, March 2006.
17   "Continues to manipulate": International Crisis Group report, 6.
17   Minnawi's life: Prunier, 182-183.
17   "No cohesive command": Gen. Martin Luther Agwei, quoted in UN news release issued August 12, 2008.
17   "I strongly condemn": UN High Commissioner for Human Rights news release, July 10, 2008, 1.

Chapter Two: The People

19   "The Lion, Hyena, and Fox were friends": Beaton, 146-150.
19-21   Major tribes of the South and North: *Encyclopedia Britannica Online*.
19   "Celebrated breakthrough": news release, Abyei Chamber of Commerce, April 15, 2007.

19   Abyei burned: "Abandoning Abyei," Human Rights Watch, July 2008.

20   "Ethnic identity": *Encyclopedia Britannica Online*, "The Sudan."

20   "Peace villages": Polgreen, July 22, 2007.

20   "Most Nuba were not happy": Mohammed, August 12, 2008.

21   "Conveniently distant, weak and safely nonwhite" and "Indignant" Europe: Hochschild, 28 and 92.

22-24   "Saba Recalls Life From 'Before'" and "A Northern Story": Beher, adapted from field reporting for UMCOR, 2005. Versions of these stories were published in 2006 as "Harvest and Hope Mark UMCOR's First Year in Sudan."

24   Darfur village governance: Hari, 34.

25   "When the government": Hari, 192.

25   Dwellings and farming practices, Beher field notes, 2005.

26   "Seventeen kilometers to draw water": UMCOR DVD, 2007.

26-27   Rape as weapon of war: UNHCHR, January 27, 2006, 12.

26   Effects of rape: Smith-Spark, BBC news release, December 8, 2004.

27   Vulnerable to abuses: Human Rights Watch, April 2008, 17.

27   Range of gender violence: Human Rights Watch, April 2008, 11.

27-31   Primer on Islam: I.A. Ibrahim, 45-48; 65-67.

31-32   Missionary activity in Sudan: Operation Nehemiah, http://www.wenderdemo web site.

32-33   Holston Conference covenant: Spence, *UM News Service*, February 26, 2008.

33   A barrier of trash: Beher, field notes, August 2005.

33   "Eight-foot high grass": Dau, 18.

34-35   The camps: Beher, adapted from field reporting for UMCOR, 2005. A version of this story was published in 2006 as "Harvest and Hope Mark UMCOR's First Year in Sudan."

Chapter Three: The Politics of War & Peace

37   "A long-running political battle": Prunier, 82-87.

38-40   Global climate change, failed counterinsurgency, ethnic cleansing: Prunier, 102-105.

38   Eighteen-month study: Borger, June 23, 2007.

39   "Climate of complete contradiction": Prunier, 109.

39   "Not a coherent horror": Prunier, 110.

39   "The world's greatest humanitarian crisis": Kapila, quoted in Prunier, 127.

40-41   The tragedy of colonial rule: Kolawole, 3, 12.

40   "Nativized elite": Prunier, 7.

41   "Sudanization": Flint and de Waal, 14.

41   "Dominion by violence": Amadiume, 100.

41   Displacement: *CIA Factbook*, May 2008.

42   Climate change: UNEP news release, June 22, 2007.

42   Over-centralization of Khartoum: Flint and de Waal, 29.

42   Flood of guns from Libya: Prunier, 59.

43   Women's issues in Darfur: Muhammad, 5.

43-44 Famine's effect on Nimeiri government: Flint and de Waal, 48.

43   Sidebar material: Muhammad, 6.

44-47 "The myths of war": Wax, April 23, 2006.

44   "All Darfurians are Muslim": Flint and de Waal, 10.

45   "Turabi headed an Islamist approach": de Waal, from *The Nation*, March 19, 2007, page 2.

45   China as oil buyer and developer: Engdahl, from *Asian Times*, May 30, 2007, page 3.

46   Leverage of oil investments: Malcorra, quoted in MacFarquhar, "Why Darfur Still Bleeds," in *The New York Times*, July 13, 2008.

46   Proxy war: Flint and de Waal, 55.

47   "Morality one-upsmanship": Dealy, 10.

47   Peace appears to mean subjugation: Flint and de Waal, 133.

48   Juan E. Méndez comments: Amnesty USA news feed, April 13, 2007.

49-50 "If this generation": Louanchi, 2008 conversation reported to the author by Else Adjali, former General Board of Global Ministries representative to the United Nations.

50   "Oil in Sudan": Ziada, 6.

50   Regime change theory: Engdahl, page 5 of 7.

50-51 Rony Brauman dissent: Armanios, *Human Rights Tribune*, March 13, 2008.

51   Trafficking: United States State Department, "Trafficking in Persons" report issued June 12, 2007.

51   "No more saviors": Iweala, July 24, 2007.

52   Comprehensive Peace Agreement highlights: http://www.iss.co.za/AF/profiles/Sudan/darfur/cpaprov.htm.

53   Comprehensive Peace Agreement neither comprehensive nor consensus: Polgreen, *The New York Times*, May 4, 2006.

53   "A weak paper bulwark": Prunier, 179.

Chapter Four: The Dream of Peace

55   "Those we left behind": Beher, UMCOR Sudan series, 2006.

55   Major political parties: Sudan.net, May 27, 2007.

56   "So far as it depends on you": Romans 12:18, NRSV.

56   "God calls oppressed people for freedom": Cone, 189-196

56-57 Black church response and exhortations: *Religion News Service*, September 1, 2005, and May 1, 2008.

57-59 Truth and reconciliation process analysis: Hauss, 2005.

59-60 Sharia law summary: Feldman, March 16, 2008.

60   Number of humanitarian aid workers: Perttula, June 2008.

61   "We are all Sudanese": Beher, field notes, August 2005.

62-64 "People's need and people driven": Beher, adapted from field reporting for UMCOR, 2005. A version of this story was published in 2006 as "Harvest and Hope Mark UMCOR's First Year in Sudan."

64   "A church of servants": Beher, adapted from news release for UMCOR, October 2006.

65   Covenant of Holston Conference and East Africa Conference: Spence, February 26, 2008.

66-68   "Victor Chol: Lost Boy No More": Beher, interviews and emails with V. Chol, May 13, 2008.

67   "War over a handful of corn": Kapucsinski, 198.

67   Sudanese entrepreneur envisions economic development: Mo Ibrahim Foundation Index, 2007.

67-68   Plans of Sudanese Lost Boys and Girls Volunteer Association: Chol, May 13, 2008.

68   "Duk County Rebuilds": Dau, 264.

68-69   "Peace is in our hands": UNESCO for the International Decade of Peace, 2001.

Chapter Five: The Church's Moral Authority and Sudan's Dream of Peace

71-76   United Methodist reports and resolution on Sudan: General Conference, April 2008.

77   Bush signs divestment bill: Stolberg in *The New York Times*, Jan. 1, 2008, A-7.

77   "A proven tool": NAACP web site, 2007.

77   "Higher aim": Osman, 2.

77   "As efficient. But silent": Polgreen et al, July 15, 2008, *New York Times*. In some editions Luis Moreno-Ocampo was quoted as saying that President al-Bashir's choices of weapons (rape, violent suppression of a counter-insurgency) were as efficient as more overt weapons of war but silent.

78   Sustainable peace: Lewis for KAIROS, February 2007.

79   Replacing infrastructure a 15-hour-a-day job: Beher, field notes, August 2005.

79   "Educate a woman": Beher, field notes, August 2005.

79-80   Worth of women's lives: Dau, 24.

80   How Sudanese women exercise leadership: Kolawole, 13, 29, 78.

80-81   Women's right to criticize: Muhammad, 2 ff.

81   "Domestic and production roles": Muhammad, 1.

81   Survey data and women's roles in Sudan: Otto and Chambers, abstracts for Sudan Studies Association, May 2008.

81   Leadership through dignity; story of Haja Nasra: Muhammad, 8.

81   Parable of the uncaring judge: Matthew 18:2-5, NRSV.

81   "Between hope and despair": WCC, May 19, 2006.

81   "A better future": WCC news release by J. Michel, July 31, 2008.

82-83   "Culture of accountability": UNCHCR, 41.

83-84   Indigenous communities: Elbashir, quoted by Liebling, June 29, 2005, 4.

85   "Peace will not come in isolation": Ismail, in "Sudan Peace and Democracy Watch," February 28, 2008. Retrieved from Center for American Progress, http://www.americanprogress.org/issues/2008/02/sudan_peace.html .

85   "Long is the absence of light/that paints things awake": Al-Raddi, from *The Guardian*, tr. Hafiz Kheir and Sarah Maguire, October 2006.

89   Timeline: Adapted from *Christian Science Monitor*, September 12, 2005.

Bibliography

Al-Raddi, Al-Siddiq. "A Monkey at the Window." Translated from the Arabic by Hafiz Kheir and Sarah Maguire. Retrieved Aug. 12, 2008, from http://image.guardian.co.uk/sys-files/Books/documents/2006/10/16/monkey.pdf .

Amadiume, Ifi. *Reinventing Africa: Matriarchy, Religion and Culture*. London: Zed Books, Ltd., 1997.

Armanios, Rachad. "Genocide in Darfur? No, It's about oil," in *Human Rights Tribune*, March 13, 2008. Retrieved from http://www.humanrights-geneva.info/Genocide-in-Darfur-No-it-s-about,2871.

Beaton, A.C. "Tigri Folk-Tales," from *Sudan Notes and Records*, Volume XXVII, 1947, pages 146-150. Retrieved from http://awkir.com/tigri_folktales.htm .

Beher, Linda. Field notes, Khartoum and South Darfur, Sudan, August 2005.

_____. Interview notes and email exchange with Victor Chol, May 13, 2008.

_____. "Harvest and Hope Mark UMCOR's First Year in Sudan." Field reporting from Khartoum and South Darfur. Retrieved from http://new.gbgm-umc.org/umcor/work/fieldoffices/news/archives06/sudan3/ .

Borger, Julian. "Darfur Conflict Heralds Era of Wars Triggered by Climate Change, UN Report Warns," in *The Guardian*, June 23, 2007. Retrieved from http://www.guardian.co.uk/environment/2007/jun/23/sudan.climatechange/ .

Brinkhoff, Thomas. City Population. Sudan information compiled from Ministry of Council of Ministers, Central Bureau of Statistics, Sudan. Retrieved from http://www.citypopulation.de/cities.html .

Bul Dau, John, with Michael S. Sweeney. *God Grew Tired of Us*. Washington, DC: National Geographic Society, first paperback printing 2008.

Chambers, Sacha; Green, Datejie; Muhammad, Baqie Badawi; and Otto, Margaret. From Sudan Studies Association Call for Papers, 27th Annual Conference, May 16-18, 2008. Retrieved from http://www.sudanstudies.org/ .

Chol, Victor. "Sudanese Lost Boys and Girls Volunteer Association Plans." Document emailed to author May 13, 2008.

Christian Science Monitor. "Timeline: Sudan's Long Path From War to Peace." September 12, 2005. Retrieved from http://www.csmonitor.com/2005/0912/p10s01-woaf.html .

CIA Factbook. May 2008. Retrieved from https://www.cia.gov/library/publications/the-world-factbook/geos/su.html .

Comprehensive Peace Agreement Summary. Retrieved from http://www.iss.co.za/AF/profiles/Sudan/darfur/cpa-prov.htm .

Cone, James H. *God of the Oppressed*, revised edition. Maryknoll, New York: Orbis Books, 1997.

Davis, Kimberly. "The Truth About Slavery in Sudan." *Ebony*, August 2001. Retrieved from http://findarticles.com/p/articles/mi_m1077/is_10_56/ai_76770615 .

Dealey, Sam. "An Atrocity That Needs No Exaggeration." From *The New York Times* "Week in Review," Sunday, August 12, 2007.

Dinka (2008), in *Encyclopedia Britannica*. Retrieved June 17, 2008, from *Encyclopedia Britannica Online*: http://www.britannica.com/eb/article-9030507 .

Engdahl, F. William. "Darfur: Forget Genocide, There's Oil." From *Asia Times Online*, May 25, 2007. Retrieved from http://www.atimes.com/atimes/China_Business/IE25Cb04.html .

Feldman, Noah. "Why Sharia?" From *The New York Times Magazine*, March 16, 2008, pages 46-51.

Fisher, Jonah. "South Sudan's Unlikely Capital." From BBC News, January 21, 2005. Retrieved from http://www.news.bbc.co.uk/go/pr/fr/-/1/hi/world/africa/4192133.stm .

Flint, Julie and Alex de Waal. *Darfur: A Short History of a Long War*. London: Zed Books, 2005.

Hari, Daoud. *The Translator: A Tribesman's Memoir of Darfur*. New York: Random House, 2008.

Hochschild Adam. *King Leopold's Ghost: A Story of Greed, Terror and Heroism in Colonial Africa*. New York: Houghton Mifflin, Mariner Books Edition, 1999.

Human Rights Watch. *Abandoning Abyei: Destruction and Displacement*. July 2008, 1-32.

_____. *Five Years On: No Justice for Sexual Violence in Darfur*. April 2006, 6-36.

Ibrahim, I.A. *A Brief Illustrated Guide to Understanding Islam,* second edition. Houston, Texas: Darussalam Publishers, 1997.

International Monetary Fund. "Statement by the World Bank, the UN and the IMF on Sudan." Jointly issued news release #06-50, March 10, 2006. Retrieved from http://www.imf.org/external/np/sec/pr/2006/pr0650.htm .

Ismail, Omer. "Sudan Peace and Democracy Watch." Center for American Progress, February 28, 2008. Retrieved from http://www/americanprogress.org/issues/2008/02/sudan_peace.html .

Iweala, Uzodinma. "An African's Plea: No More 'Saviors.'" From *The Washington Post*, July 24, 2007.

Joshua Project, "Ethnic People Groups of Sudan," retrieved from http://www.joshuaproject.net/countries. php?rog3=SU .

Kapuscinski, Ryszard. *The Shadow of the Sun*. Tr. Klara Glowczewska. New York: Vintage Books, a division of Random House, Inc., 2001.

Kolawole, Mary E. Modupe. *Womanism and African Consciousness*. Trenton, NJ: Africa World Press, Inc., 1997.

Lewis, John. "Seven Steps for Peace in Darfur." Policy Briefing Paper, #7, February 2007. KAIROS. Toronto, Canada. Retrieved from http://www.kairoscanada.org/e/countries/sudan/index.asp .

MacFarquahar, Neil. "Why Darfur Still Bleeds." From *The New York Times*, July 13, 2008. Retrieved from http://www.nytimes.com/2008/07/13/weekinreview/13macfarquhar.html?pagewanted=print .

McFague, Sallie. *Super, Natural Christians: How We Should Love Nature*. Minneapolis: Fortress Press, 1997.

Mohammed, Hafiz. "The Risk of Rebellion in Kordofan." From Africa Files, posted August 12, 2008. Retrieved from http://www.africafiles.org/database/ .

Muhammad, Baqie Badawi. "Famine, Women Creative Acts, and Gender Dynamics in Manawashai, Darfur, Western Sudan." From *Jenda: A Journal of Culture and African Women Studies* (2002), retrieved from http://www.jendajournal.com/vol12.1/muhammad.html .

NAACP. "Support for Divestment from Sudan." From NAACP web site, December 19, 2007. Retrieved from http://www.naacp.org/get-involved/activism/alerts/110thaa/2007-12-19/DARFUR.DIVESTMENT.On.to.the. President.pdf .

Operation Nehemiah. "Christian Church History in the Sudan." Retrieved from http://www.operationsnehemiah. org/page/Christian-Church-History-in-the-Sudan .

Orimalade, Adesola. "Price of Peace in Africa: Agreement in Sudan Between Government and Rebel." From *Journal of Turkish Weekly Opinion*, February 11, 2005. Retrieved from http://www.turkishweekly.net/comments. php?id=185 .

Osman, Salih Mahmoud. "Justice and Peace in Darfur." *The Nation*, March 7, 2007. Retrieved from www. thenation.com/docprint.mhtml?i=20070319&s=osman .

Perttula, Kent. "A Guide to Humanitarian and Development Efforts of InterAction Member Agencies in Sudan and Chad," June 2008. Retrieved from http://www.interaction.org/files.cgi/6308_2008_SUDAN_AND_CHAD. pdf.

Polgreen, Lydia. "A Godsend for Darfur, or a Curse?" *The New York Times Week in Review*, July 22, 2007, Section 4, Pages 1 and 12.

_____. "An Incomplete Peace: Sudan's Never-Ending War With Itself." *The New York Times*, May 4, 2006. Retrieved from http://www.nytimes.com/2006/05/04/world/africa/04darfur.html?_r=1&scp=1&sq=Lydia+Polgreen+An+Incomplete+Peace&st=nyt&oref=slogin .

_____. "Arrest Is Sought of Sudan Leader in Genocide Case." Reported with Marlise Simons and Jeffrey Gettleman. *The New York Times*, July 15, 2008. Retrieved from http://www.nytimes.com/2008/07/15/world/africa/15sudan.html?ref=world .

Prunier, Gerard. *Darfur: The Ambiguous Genocide*. Ithaca, NY: Cornell University Press, 2005.

_____. "Did Somebody Say Genocide?" From "The Politics of Death in Darfur," from *Current History*, May 2006, reprinted *Harper's Magazine*, August 2006.

Relief Web. Maps of Sudan and Darfur, retrieved from http://www.reliefweb.int/rw/dbc.nsf/doc104?OpenForm&rc=1&cc=sdn .

Rieff, David. "Good vs. Good in Darfur." From *The Los Angeles Times*, June 24, 2007. Retrieved from http://www.latimes.com/news/opinion/la-op-rieff24jun24,0,4338046.story .

Salopek, Paul. "Lost in the Sahel." From *National Geographic*, April 2008. Pages 34-67.

Smith, Jane I. *Islam in America*. New York: Columbia University Press, 1999.

Smith-Spark, Laura. "How Did Rape Become a Weapon of War?" From BBC News, August 12, 2004. Retrieved from http://news.bbc.co.uk/go/pr/fr/-/2/hi/in_depth/4078677.stm .

Spence, Annette. "Holston, East Africa Conferences Sign Sudan Covenant." *United Methodist News Service* news release, issued February 26, 2008. Retrieved from http://www.umc.org/site/apps/nlnet/content3.aspx?c=lwL4KnN1LtH&b=2433457&ct=5060515 .

The Sudan (2008). In *Encyclopedia Britannica Online*. Retrieved June 17, 2008, from *Encyclopedia Britannica Online*: http://www.britannica.com/eb/article-24336 ; http://www.britannica.com/eb/article-24366 ; and http://www.britannica.com/eb/article-24342 .

Sudan Experience. "Negotiations of the Comprehensive Peace Process: Questions for Participants. Retrieved from http://www.adst.org/sep/questions2.htm .

Sudan.net. "Major Sudanese Political Parties." Retrieved from http://www.sudan.net/government/parties.html .

UMCOR. "Gifts of Hope: UMCOR in Darfur." DVD, © 2007 General Board of Global Ministries.

United Methodist reports, resolutions, and statements on Darfur/Sudan, from General Conferences 2004 and 2008. Full texts at http://www.umc.org/site/c.lwL4KnN1LtH/b.3989461/k.1E85/General_Conference_2008.htm .

United Nations Development Programme. "Abyei Chamber of Commerce: The Union of Dinka and Misseryia Traders." News release, April 15, 2007. Retrieved from http://www.sd.undp.org/Presspdf/Abyei%20Chamber%20 of%20commerce.pdf .

United Nations Environmental Programme. "Environmental Degradation Triggering Tensions and Conflict in Sudan." News release issued June 2007. Retrieved from http://www.unep.org/Documents.Multilingual/Default. Print.asp?DocumentID=512&articleID=5621&1=en .

UNESCO. "Mainstreaming the Culture of Peace." Brochure published as a global action plan for the Decade of Peace, 2001-2010, retrieved from http://unesdoc.unesco.org/images/0012/001263/126398e.pdf .

United Nations High Commissioner for Human Rights. "Second Periodic Report on the Human Rights Situation in Sudan." Issued January 27, 2006. Retrieved from http://www.ohchr.org/EN/Countries/AfricaRegion/Pages/ SDPeriodicReports.aspx .

United Nations High Commissioner for Human Rights. "UN Expert on the Situation of Human Rights in Sudan Concludes Visit." News release dated July 10, 2008. Retrieved from http://www.unhchr.ch/ .

United Nations Millennium Development Project. Information retrieved from http://www.unmillenniumproject. org/index.htm .

United Nations News Center. "Rebel Groups Must Unite to Reach Lasting Solution for Darfur." News release issued August 12, 2008. Retrieved from http://www.un.org/apps/news/story.asp?NewsID=27683&Cr=unamid&Cr1.

United States State Department. "Trafficking in Persons Report." Issued by the Office to Monitor and Combat Trafficking in Persons, June 12, 2007. Retrieved from http://www.state.gov/g/tip/rls/tiprpt/2007/82807.htm .

de Waal, Alex. "The Wars of Sudan." From *The Nation*, March 19, 2007. Retrieved from http://www.thenation. com/doc/20070319/de_waal .

Wax, Emily. "Five Truths About Darfur." From *The Washington Post*, Sunday April 23, 2006. Page B3.

Wikipedia. "Darfur." Retrieved from http://en.wikipedia.org/wiki/Darfur .

World Council of Churches. "Executive Committee Statement on Sudan." Issued at Geneva May 19, 2006. Retrieved from http://www.oikoumene.org/index.php?id=2260 .

_____. "Peace in Sudan May Take a Long Time." Interview with Marina Peter by Juan Michel. World Council of Churches feature released July 31, 2008. Retrieved from http://overcomingviolence.org/news-and-events/news/ dov-news-english/article/1298/peace-in-sudan-may-take-a.html .

Study Guide
By Maxine West

Forward

The Beauty and Courage of Sudan: Why a Dream of Peace Is Possible is the geographical mission study written by Linda Beher. Sudan, the largest country of the African continent, is experiencing enormous political and sociological transition. Since its independence 52 years ago, Sudan has suffered two civil wars, severe drought, famine, and widespread displacement of civilians. The two military conflicts have produced a nation divided, North against South, Arabs against black Africans, and Muslims against non-Muslim religions. Even as we prepare for this study, the crisis in the Western region of Darfur is threatening yet a third round of military conflict.

The timeliness of this study is no accident. The crisis in Darfur has captured international interest and concern since early 2004 when the United Nations named Darfur as the worst humanitarian situation in the world. In March 2005, the United Methodist Committee on Relief (UMCOR) joined with other international aid organizations providing humanitarian assistance, with operations in Darfur and an office in Khartoum, the capital of Sudan. Since February 2006, UMCOR programs and efforts in South Sudan have focused on repatriation and reintegration of people returning to the region after years of war; training 3,600 farmers to help them improve their agricultural techniques and increase crop production; providing training to teacher associations; and the implementation of the Child Protection and Development Program, providing services for internally displaced women and children.

Despite the wars and military conflicts, food and water shortages, climatic changes, and displacement of thousands of people who called Sudan their home, at the core of this vast country are beauty and an enormous spirit of hospitality and courage. This study is an opportunity to explore something of the core, the beauty, and the courage of Sudan, a place so ancient yet so full of modern contradictions. We hope to learn about the why, where, how, who, and what that form the core issues of this place that is, if not the very heart of Africa itself, the embodiment of many of the issues of the 21st century continent of Africa. Finally, we hope to learn why the beauty, hospitality, and courage of the Sudanese people promise the hope that eventually the dream of peace will be realized there.

Introduction

This study guide is designed to assist leaders in facilitating the geographical mission study on Sudan. The study invites participants to:

- Examine briefly the historical roots of Sudan in an effort to understand the conflicts between the Northern and Southern regions of the country;
- Listen to the voices of Sudanese people in their struggles for independence and peace;
- Explore critical issues: health, food, water, and sustainability that challenge and threaten life in the region.
- Explore peace and reconciliation efforts in Sudan.
- Examine factors and major issues leading to the ongoing destructive military conflict in Darfur and regional and international efforts to resolve them;
- Analyze peace-building models of nongovernmental organizations;
- Explore how we, as a Christian community, can work for peace and reconciliation in the Sudan region.

The situation in all of Sudan in 2008, when this study was being written, was quite volatile. Destructive armed conflict in Darfur continues despite regional and international efforts to put an end to it. The security situation remains precarious even with the presence of United Nations peacekeepers in the region. For these reasons and many more, the reader will be challenged to:

- Approach this study with loving eyes and open minds;
- Set aside any racial and religious prejudices and stereotypes that may distort their understanding of Africa in general;
- Listen to a variety of viewpoints before coming to conclusions about the people and the situation in Sudan.

Sudanese, in all of Sudan, are hopeful that, one day, peace and reconciliation will be a reality in their nation, and all people will be able to return to their ancestral homes. This is also our hope and dream as we engage in this study.

Advance Preparation

Regardless of whether you will be leading this study in a four-day school of Christian mission, a shorter mission event, a district mission event, a local unit, or a churchwide setting, advance preparation is critical.

- Be spiritually prepared. Pray for yourself and for your class participants.
- Read and reread the entire text and study guide as often as necessary to become familiar with the study and class activities.
- Set realistic objectives for each session based on the goals of the study.

If you have the option, contact class participants via mail or e-mail prior to the first class session. Introduce yourself and ask them to join you in prayer for the study. Request that they bring to the first session any recent newspaper or magazine articles about Darfur or Sudan in general; mementos from a trip to Africa; or African music CDs.

- Assemble your own collection of African memorabilia, posters, maps of Africa and Sudan, national flag of Sudan, and other materials to create a colorful and inviting visual learning space.
- Order any books and audiovisual resources recommended for the study. Allow ample time for the resources to reach you.
- Other resources you will need include Bibles, the Qur'an, *The United Methodist Hymnal, The Faith We Sing, Global Praise 1, Africa Praise Songbook*

and the CD, *Africa – Praise I, Response* and *New World Outlook* magazines, *When Freedom? Sudan in Captivity* DVD, and the mission study map, *Map & Facts: Sudan.*

- Prepare a list of Internet websites that contain additional resources and useful information on Sudan and related topics. If you plan to have participants do a project using one of the suggested sites and Internet access is not available, arrange to download and print a hard copy of the relevant material for use in the class.

Methodology

As study leader/facilitator your role is to create a safe, informal, friendly environment conducive to adult learning. Participation is a key factor in this process. To enhance individual participation and group interaction, a variety of teaching/learning techniques have been incorporated in the study guide. Each session includes exercises and options that engage as many of the five senses as possible: visualization through pictures, maps, and charts; verbal presentation through personal interviews; worship experiences, hands-on activities, and World Wide Web surfing; recordings of African music; and cultural experiences through singing.

Classroom Set-up

Consider the space you will be using. The ideal setting is a room with movable chairs, several tables, a chalkboard, newsprint, and any audiovisual equipment you plan to use. Make the space as comfortable as possible and allow room for ease of movement and small group activities. If you are meeting in a room with fixed furniture, like a sanctuary or auditorium, try to make the space conducive to learning by creating colorful tabletop displays and posters. Use African fabric on the worship center along with other African artifacts.

- World Wide Web access is desired, although not required, for class sessions. The situation in Sudan is evolving daily and the Internet offers the most current and relevant resources to supplement the study.
- Prepare colorful wall displays of a variety of visuals including photos of African scenes and images, maps, the national flag of Sudan, and colorful African fabric.
- Create a display of United Methodist Committee on Relief (UMCOR) programs and projects in Sudan. (See http://new.gbgm-umc.org/umcor/work/fieldoffices/Sudan).
- Arrange a small table holding books and other resources related to the study.
- Create a worship center for the duration of the study.
- Prepare a table display of African artifacts, mementos, and instruments collected by you and members of the class.

Planning the Study

This guide is written primarily for four two-hour sessions. However, a one-hour session option has been added for those leading a one-day study. Each session includes a wide variety of exercises and activities, so pick and choose those activities and learning opportunities most appropriate for your group and the time available.

- Develop a lesson plan for the entire study. Include approximate times and materials needed for each activity. Be as specific as necessary.
- Worship should be an integral part of the study. Create a worship center for the duration of the study. You may want to add elements to the worship center each day. Begin and close each session with prayer or a brief worship service. Use the worship resources

printed in the guide at the beginning and end of the sessions or develop your own worship material.

- Prepare hand-outs for participants. Include the purpose of the study, a brief course outline with objectives for each session, assignments, and instructions for group activities when needed.

- If possible, arrange for computer and Internet connection in the classroom. Print a list of websites to be viewed and used by participants.

- Secure all supplies and materials needed for each session, including markers, newsprint, construction paper, scissors, tape, poster boards, etc.

- Prepare a timeline of the important events in the history of Sudan. Use the information in **Appendix A, A Chronology of Key Events in Sudan**. Print the chronology on shelf paper or construction paper. Use large print so that the chronology can be read from a distance.

One-Session Study

Objectives
- To introduce the study of Sudan;
- To examine possible causes for the war in Darfur;
- To explore peace resolutions and reconciliation efforts to rebuild Sudan.

Required Materials and Supplies
- Bibles
- Qur'an
- Basic text, *The Beauty and Courage of Sudan: Why a Dream of Peace Is Possible*, by Linda Beher
- *The United Methodist Hymnal, Global Praise 1*, and *Africa Praise Songbook*
- *Map & Facts: Sudan*
- Copies of *Response* and *New World Outlook* magazines
- Newsprint, markers, and tape
- TV monitor with DVD/VCR, or LCD projector
- CD player

Preparation and Room Set-up
- Read the complete text and study guide.
- Create a worship center using suggestions found in the session plan.
- Make the room as conducive to adult learning as possible. Review suggestions found in the session plan.
- Display a collection of current news articles about Sudan and Darfur.
- Display the maps, flag, and timeline of Sudan.
- Decide how you will present the study. Below are several options for presenting the study in a single session.
    1. **Speaker:** Invite someone who is knowledgeable about Sudan.
    2. **Magazine and book reviews:** *New World Outlook* and *Response* will have articles related to the study.
    3. **Panel discussion:** Organize a panel discussion on major issues raised in the study.
    4. **Simulated radio interviews with displaced Sudanese persons.** (See **Appendix D** of the study guide.)
    5. **Show a DVD/video:** Select audiovisual resources available for this geographical study on Sudan.

Opening Worship (10 minutes)
Select one of the opening worship services found in the session plan or prepare your own. Incorporate African hymns and musical instruments in the worship experience.

Community Building (20 minutes)
In groups of three, ask participants to introduce themselves (if they do not already know each other) and then have them respond to the following questions:

- What have you recently read or heard about Sudan?
- Have you, or do you know persons who have, traveled to Africa? If yes, what were your (or their) impressions of the people and places visited?
- What are your expectations for this study?

After everyone has had a chance to respond, share responses with the total group.

Presentation of the Sudan Study (35 minutes)
Option 1: Invite a Speaker
- To invite a staff person from UMCOR, contact UMCOR, The General Board of Global Ministries, Room 330, 475 Riverside Drive, New York, NY 10115; 212-870-3909.
- Be sure the speaker understands who the audience is and what you want the speaker to address in her or

his presentation. You should also communicate the amount of time they will have for the presentation.

Option 2: Magazine and Book Reviews

- If you decide to present the study by having several persons conduct book or magazine reviews, give them the articles and books in advance so they have ample time to prepare the reviews. *Response* and *New World Outlook* magazines will have several articles related to the study.
- Ask four persons to prepare a review of the basic text, *The Beauty and Courage of Sudan* by Linda Beher. Each person will review a different chapter and summarize some of the major issues raised in the text.
- Ask one person to review and summarize ways The United Methodist Church is making a difference in Sudan. Include United Methodist Committee on Relief (UMCOR) programs and projects.

Option 3: Panel Discussion of Major Issues

- Ask several persons to participate in a panel to present major issues presented in the study regarding the conflict in Darfur. Issues to be discussed include:
  1. Global Climate Change
  2. Failed Counterinsurgency
  3. Ethnic Cleansing
  4. Colonial Occupation
- In addition to a panel, you might want to ask several individuals to prepare brief reports on issues they found interesting in the study.

Option 4: Simulated Radio Interviews

- Use the interviews printed in **Appendix D** for simulated radio interviews of displaced Sudanese persons. Ask for volunteers to assume the roles of reporter and interviewees.
- Follow the interviews with a discussion of the issues raised by the interviewees.

Option 5: Audiovisual Resources

- Review all audiovisual resources available for the study in advance.
- Show DVDs/videos available for the study.
- Prepare a series of questions for discussion following the viewing of the audiovisuals.

Discussion (20 minutes)

Regardless of the option (or combination of options) chosen for presenting the study, allow time for discussion and any actions your group might take in response to the study. As Facilitator, you will want to lead the group in a discussion of *"Next Steps: What Can We Do From Here?"* (See Chapter Five, page 71).

Closing Worship (5 minutes)

Choose one of the closing worship services in the session plan.

Four-Session Study
Session 1: A Sense of Place

Objectives
To set the stage for the study.

- To explore a brief history of Sudan.
- To discover factors leading to disputes between North and South Sudan.
- To begin to understand the insurgency in Darfur.

Required Materials and Supplies
- A few Bibles for those who did not bring their own.
- A copy of the basic text, *The Beauty and Courage of Sudan: Why a Dream of Peace is Possible*, by Linda Beher.
- A copy of *The United Methodist Hymnal*, *Africa Praise Songbook*, and *Global Praise 1*.
- An assortment of color markers, newsprint, construction paper, and non-toxic magic markers.
- An assortment of multicolored 3" x 5" index cards.
- CD player.
- A copy of the **Sudan Facts Match Game** for each participant (See **Appendix B**).
- Computer and Internet connection (if possible).
- Screen and LCD projector.

Preparation and Room Set-up
1. Prepare a worship center consisting of a Bible, one white candle, a pitcher or bowl of water, appropriate African art. Drape the table with African fabric.
2. Display the chronology of the history of Sudan along with the *Map & Facts: Sudan* and the information printed on the back of the map.
3. On a poster or newsprint, display **Sudan Fast Facts** adapted from the May 2008 *CIA Fact Book* found in Chapter One, page 15 of the text. (This information will be used to complete the **Sudan Facts Match Game**, printed in **Appendix B**).
4. In preparation for the Bible study on the good Samaritan, divide a sheet of newsprint or a poster into four equal columns. Label each column as follows: **VICTIMS; PASSERSBY; NEIGHBORS; INNKEEPERS.** Display this item on the wall for easy access throughout the study.
5. Divide the classroom into four sections representing pre-19th , 19th-, 20th-, and 21st-century Sudan.
6. Prepare colorful displays of photos, scenes, and important facts pertaining to each century. (Sources of photos: old issues of *Response*, *New World Outlook*, and *National Geographic* magazines; and tourist travel agencies.)
7. Have recorded African music playing as participants arrive for the session.
8. Check the Internet daily for updated information on the situation in Sudan.

Group Activity #1: Sudan Facts Match Game (15 minutes)
As participants arrive, give them a copy of the **Sudan Facts Match Game**. Inform them that answers to the game can be found among the resources displayed in the classroom and in Chapter One of the basic text. Allow them 15 minutes to work on the game. If they do not complete the game in the time allotted, have them complete it later.

Introductions (15 minutes)
Introduce yourself and then have participants introduce themselves. Introductions should include participants' name, church, conference, and any particular knowledge about Sudan from travels or recent articles. Ask them to briefly describe any artifacts they have brought to share with the group.

Facilitator: Overview of Study (10 minutes)
Include in the introduction:

- Organization of basic text and study guide;
- Purpose and goals of the study;
- Other primary resources; and
- Group expectations.

Opening Worship (15 minutes)

Bible Study and Reflection: Luke 10:25-37, The Parable of the Good Samaritan

Facilitator: Ask for a volunteer to read Luke 10:25-37 as participants follow along in their Bibles. In your own words, summarize the message Jesus was teaching, and identify the major four actors or characters in the parable. (**Refer to the newsprint or poster you prepared for this Bible study**). Then divide the class into six small groups and have them discuss the parallels between the parable and the situation in Sudan today. Using the multicolored index cards provided, have each group identify the following actors or characters in the Sudan scenario as assigned:

Groups 1 and 2:	Victims (blue cards)
Group 3:	Passersby (yellow cards)
Groups 4 and 5:	Neighbors (green cards)
Group 6:	Innkeepers (white cards)

Print one name per card and tape the cards under the appropriate columns of the prepared display. As the study progresses, we will identify more actors in the continuing Sudan story to be added to the display.

Hymn: "Jesu, Jesu," (stanzas 1, 2, and 3), *The United Methodist Hymnal*, #432

Prayer: God of many names, who calls us by one name, be present among us as we begin to study and learn about the peoples and situations in faraway Sudan. Enfold us with your love and compassion, and unite us with your Holy Spirit. Give us eyes to see your face and ears to hear your voice in the struggles and adversities of your people in all of Sudan. Guide our thoughts and actions in ways that bring honor and glory to you always. In Jesus' name, we pray. Amen.

Group Activity #2: The Land and Its People — Show-and-Tell (20 minutes)

Facilitator: Have participants remain in their small groups and select a recorder. Each group will be given one of the assignments listed below. Instruct them to use the mission study *Map & Facts: Sudan*, data on the back of the map, information in Chapter One of the text, and **Sudan Facts and Figures** printed in **Appendix C** to complete the assignment. Allot 10 minutes for this activity. When all groups have finished, have reporters print their findings on newsprint to share with the entire class. Ask recorders to use the map of Sudan to locate cities and regions included in their reports as appropriate.

Group 1:	What is the estimated population of Sudan? Name the capital and principal cities of Sudan. Name the countries that border Sudan.
Group 2:	What is the total area of Sudan? Name and briefly describe the four main geographical regions comprising Sudan.
Group 3:	Name and describe Sudan's most dominant geographical feature. What are some of the other major rivers and waterways that flow through Sudan?
Group 4:	Name the principal ethnic groups, religions, and languages in Sudan. List the percentage of: (1) each group in the population; (2) each religious affiliation; and

(3) each language spoken. What is the official language of the country?

Group 5: Describe the life expectancy of Sudanese. Compare the life expectancy rates of females with males. What is the education policy for children in Sudan? Find the literacy rate for Sudan. Compare literacy rates of females with males.

Group 6: Name the major sectors of the economy in Sudan. List the percentage of population engaged in each. Identify the major trading partners of Sudan. What products account for much of the export revenue? What products are imported?

Facilitator: Highlight key information about the land and its people found in the reports. Answer any questions or concerns that may arise.

Group Activity #3: A Chronology of Key Events (20 minutes)

Facilitator: Call the groups' attention to the Sudan chronology and to the way the room is divided into four sections representing key events in the history of Sudan. Inform them that for the next 20 minutes they will explore these events in order to understand some of the core issues challenging the people and endangering the land in all of Sudan. Divide the class into four groups. Each group is to examine, analyze, and discuss some of the major events of the century they are assigned. The group should select a reporter to report findings to the class. Each group is to respond to the following questions where appropriate:

• What are the key events of the particular century?

• What region of Sudan was most affected by the events?
• Who were some of the principal actors involved in the events?
• List key factors leading up to the events. Include efforts to resolve issues resulting from named events.

Facilitator: The conflicts between Northern and Southern Sudan are often understood through their historical roots: centuries of exploitation and slave-raiding by the "Arab" North against the "African" South, followed by Britain and Egyptian imperialist intervention. The crisis in Darfur has developed partly because of the incomplete resolution of these North-South wars. While religion, race, economic exploitation, and colonialism are all major elements in the crisis, none of these factors fully explain the situation apart from the deep-rooted disconnect between North and South.

In the three years of this latest confrontation in Darfur, hundreds of thousands have died and some 2.5 million have been displaced with no end to the conflict in sight. The wars in Darfur have captured the attention of Western activists and humanitarian organizations including the United Methodist Committee on Relief (UMCOR). In March 2005 UMCOR joined other international aid organizations providing humanitarian assistance, with operations in Darfur and an office in Khartoum.

In spite of signed peace agreements, humanitarian assistance, and deployment of United Nations peacekeeper forces in the region, the fighting continues in Darfur and threatens to extend into other neighboring borders. In the midst of this crisis, we stand in solidarity with our Sudanese brothers and sisters and join them in prayer that one day in the near future, peace and reconciliation will be restored in their country.

Closing Centering

Please stand and sing the African-American national anthem "Lift Every Voice and Sing," *The United Methodist Hymnal*, #519, honoring survival through slavery, racism, and intolerance.

Prayer: Let us pray,

God of love and mercy, who hears the cries of our brothers and sisters in Sudan, grant us your vision of peace and the fullness of life. We pray for the leaders and governments of both South and North Sudan that they will set aside longstanding differences and set right priorities and work to restore stability, peace, and wholeness in the region. On your healing and saving power we rely. Amen.

Assignment for Session 2

- Ask participants to read Chapters One and Two in the basic text.
- Ask someone who enjoys surfing the Internet to monitor updates on Sudan each day. A number of websites are printed in the Bibliography.
- In the next two sessions, we will listen to the voices of some of the displaced Sudanese people who dream of someday returning to their homeland. To facilitate their story, interviews will be conducted using the scripts printed in **Appendix D**. Assign volunteers to assume the following roles:
  1. **Reporter**: conducts all interviews.
  2. **Saba**; a displaced woman from a rural Zalingei village in West Darfur.
  3. **Angelina**; a resident of Julha Farms, a women's farm in Ed Daein, South Darfur.
  4. **Jane Ohuma**; UMCOR's head of mission in Sudan.
  5. **Musayahia**; a student in Khartoum.
- Ask three volunteers to make a 10-minute report on the following topics:
  1. Tribes and Social Connection (Chapter Two, pages 24-25);
  2. Occupations (Chapter Two, pages 25-26);
  3. Vulnerability of Women and Children (Chapter Two, pages 26-27);
- Ask two volunteers to prepare a presentation on the Five Pillars of Islam. Use the poster and construction paper to build and label the pillars.
- Watch a DVD or video scheduled for study during audiovisual times.

Four-Session Study
Session 2: The People of Sudan

Objectives

- To become familiar with the rich diversity among the Sudanese people—their languages and traditions.
- To learn about daily life of Sudanese people living in villages and camps for displaced persons.
- To explore the role of religion in the region.
- To examine core beliefs of Islam.

Required Materials and Supplies

- Bible
- The Qur'an
- *The United Methodist Hymnal, Africa Praise Songbook, Global Praise 1*
- An assortment of multicolored 3" x 5" index cards
- Newsprint, magic markers, tape, scissors
- An assortment of colored construction paper
- Five sheets of white poster paper
- Computer and Internet connection (if possible)

Preparation and Room Set-up

- Add the Qur'an to the worship center.
- Print the Five Articles of Faith of Islam on newsprint, or chalk or dry erase board.
- Simulate a radio station for interviews. Include a small table with an imitation mike and three chairs. Using large letters, print the name of the radio station on construction paper and attach it to the base of the mike.
- Make copies of interview scripts for radio interviews (**Appendix D**).
- Make sure Sudan chronology is posted.
- Arrange for computer and Internet connection for web research and study, if possible.
- Have recorded African music playing as class assembles for the session.

Opening Worship (20 minutes)

Hymn: "Halleluja" (stanza 1), *Global Praise 1*, #31
Call to Worship: *(Based on Psalm 24)*

Leader: The earth is the Lord's.

All: **The whole earth belongs to God, and everything in it.**

Leader: Rocks, flowers, people, land, water, nations, and cultures, are all God's creation.

All: **The whole earth belongs to God, and everything in it.**

Leader: God created, founded, and sustains the earth.

All: **Without God, there is nothing.**

Leader: Who is able to ascend the mountain of God and stand in God's holy place?

All: **Only those with clean hands and a pure heart.**

Leader: Only those who acknowledge God as creator and sustainer of the earth.

All: **Alleluia!**

Hymn: "Halleluja," (stanza 3), *Global Praise 1*, #31
Prayer: Creator and sustainer God, who formed the earth and all that is in it, open our eyes, our minds, and our hearts to recognize the signs of your creative and transforming power at work in the world. Fill us with your Holy Spirit and enable us to participate in

your works of justice, peace, healing, and reconciliation. Amen.

Group Activity #1: Tribal Tapestry of Sudan (20 minutes)

Facilitator: The commonly held image of Sudan is that of a country divided into Arab (or Muslim) and black (non-Muslim) halves in the North and the South. The reality is that there are 19 major ethnic groups in Sudan, divided into over 500 subgroups and speaking over 169 languages. In Southern Sudan alone, the five major ethnic groups speak at least 100 languages. Understanding the many groups is key to understanding Sudan and the struggles for liberation and self-governance. Divide the class into six small groups. Print the names of the following tribal groups on a separate multicolored 3" x 5" index card: Major tribes of the North (Arabs): Dinka, Nuer, Shilluk, Nuba, and Misseriya. Give each group an index card and have them research information about their assigned tribal group. Use the textbook, study guide, and other supplementary resources available in the classroom to find information about these tribal groups. Have each group record findings on newsprint to present to the entire group. Have small groups add any significant events and dates related to tribal groups to the Sudan chronology as appropriate. Use multicolored index cards to add this information.

Facilitator: Refer class to the paragraph *"What Does it Mean to be Arab in Sudan,"* page 21 in the text. Although the current conflict in Darfur has been framed as a battle between Arabs and black Africans, division between ethnic groups and the split between herders and farmers accounts for much of the dispute. Each tribe gives itself the label of "African" or "Arab" based on what language its members speak and whether they work the soil or herd livestock. Also, if they attain a certain level of wealth, they call themselves Arab.

Listen to the Voices of Africans (15 minutes):
Radio Interview: Saba and Musayahia
Reports:
1. Tribes and Social Connection (10 minutes)
2. Occupations (10 minutes)
3. Vulnerability of Women and Children (10 minutes)
4. The Role of Religions in Sudan

Group Activity #2: Major Religions in Sudan (20 minutes)

Facilitator: About 70 percent of the people of Sudan are Muslim, some 5 percent are Christians, and most of the remaining 25 percent follow traditional religions. The people of Northern Sudan are predominately Sunni Muslims (Sunni Islam), while most of the people in the South are Christians. Divide the class into 3 small groups and assign each one of the three major religions (Muslim, Christian, and traditional). Have each group record findings on newsprint for reporting to the class. Groups are to research important facts about their assigned religion including:

- When the religion first arrived in Sudan;
- Who was responsible for spreading the religion in the region;
- The role the particular religion plays in Sudanese society.

Report: *The Five Pillars of Islam (10 minutes)*
Facilitator Lead the class in a discussion of village life in Ed Daein, in North Darfur, and in the South near Yei (See Chapter Two, pages 33-34).

Closing Worship: Celebration at El Ferdous (10 minutes)

Facilitator: El Ferdous, one of five camps in South Darfur where UMCOR has programs for displaced persons, is home to some 30,000 persons. UMCOR hosts a reception center in the camp that has been described as the only "humane" reception center in the Darfur region.

New arrivals are welcomed and led through a registration process that collects information about their hometowns, their families, and their needs. They are shown to their temporary *gotia*, or houses, inside a protected compound. They will live in the *gotia* until they are assigned a permanent site on which to build a home using cut branches, grass, and reeds found near camp. Plastic sheeting and mats provided by UMCOR are also used in building these homes.

Since its installation in June 2004, the reception center has hosted some 20 to 25 households a month. Information collected at the center is shared so that the most vulnerable households can receive what they need not only from UMCOR but also from other international agencies working in the area.

In a displaced persons camp, the last thing visitors expect to find are people expressing joy. However, this is precisely what a group of visitors from the United States found upon their visit to the camp. Members of the Ohio-based Ginghamsburg United Methodist Church, were greeted with a celebration of singing, dancing, and great joy. Let us join in the celebration at El Ferdous as residents greet their guests from the United States.

Songs of Joy:

  "Tino tenda Jesu" ("Thank you, Jesus, amen"), *Global Praise 1*, #45

  "Wa wa wa emimimo" ("Come, O Holy Spirit, come"), *Global Praise 1*, #64

Scripture: Psalm 107:1-9

Litany: "Let the people know," (Based on the South Sudan hymn, "Shukuru Allah," *Global Praise 1*, #56)

Leader: Shu-ku-ru Al-lah, nih-na kul-lu moras-sa-lat,

All: **Let the people know: messengers are present here.**

Leader: Shu-ku-ru Al-lah, nih-na kul-lu moras-sa-lat,

All: **Let the people know: messengers are present here.**

Leader: nin-na kul-lu mo-ras-sa-lat lei Ye-suá.

All: **For the strength to witness we give thanks, O God.**

Songs of Joy:

  "Halleluja," *Global Praise 1*, #31
  "Siyahamba" ("We Are Marching in the Light of God"), *The Faith We Sing*, p. 2235b

Benediction:

Leader: May the God of hope walk before you to guide you, behind you to shield you, above you to bless you, beneath you to uphold you. May the peace of God be yours now and forevermore. Amen!

Assignment for Session 3

Read Chapter Three in the basic text.

- As part of session 3, an interview with Emily Wax, *The Washington Post*'s Africa bureau chief, will take place. She will be discussing, "The Myth of War" based on her article, "Five Truths About Darfur", appearing in the April 23, 2006 issue of *The Washington Post*.
- Ask a volunteer to assume the role of Emily Wax. The Facilitator will conduct the interview. Material for the interview is printed in **Appendix G** of this study guide. ("Five Truths about Darfur," *The Washington Post*, Sunday April 23, 2006, Page B3, can be retrieved by searching for Emily Wax, "Five Truths about Darfur" on the Internet.)
- Ask a volunteer to make a 10-minute report on Kairos Policy Briefing Paper No. 7, February 2007, "Seven Steps for Peace in Darfur" by John Lewis. The article can be downloaded and printed from the Internet (http://www.kairoscanada.org). The report will be presented in the fourth session.

Four-Session Study
Session 3: The Politics of War and Peace

Objectives
- To explore possible causes of the war in Darfur;
- To examine the effects of the wars in Sudan;
- To explore some of the myths of war;
- To consider some of the multinational issues at play in the recent conflict in Darfur.

Required Materials and Supplies
- Bible
- *Songs of Zion, Global Praise 1, The United Methodist Hymnal*
- Newsprint, magic markers, tape
- CD player
- Computer and Internet connection, if possible
- DVD player and monitor
- DVD *"When Freedom?/Sudan in Captivity,"* produced by Friendship Press

Preparation and Room Set-up
- To the worship center, add a small can of petroleum/ motor oil, rich soil in a small plastic bag, and cotton balls (representing some of the rich natural resources of Sudan).
- Set up the simulated radio station for interviews.
- Make copies of Interview #2.
- Make copies of **Appendix G** for interview with Emily Wax.
- Develop a chart of the "Key Issues" summarized in Chapter Three (pages 37-53 of the text) for presentation during the session.
- Check the Internet for updated news about Sudan and Darfur.
- Have recorded African music playing as participants arrive for the session.

Opening Worship: (10 minutes)
Hymn: "Alleluia," *The United Methodist Hymnal*, #186

Bible Study and Reflection: *Micah 4:1-4*

Facilitator: Ask a volunteer to read Micah 4:1-4. Then ask the class to think about the things that will make for peace in Sudan. Print their responses on newsprint.

Hymn: "Study War No More," *Songs of Zion*, #138

Prayer: God of peace and justice, strengthen us in our desire to learn the things that make for peace and to work for justice and right relations with all peoples. We hear the cries of Sudanese people who yearn to live in peace and without fear. We pray that the violence, crimes against women and children, and corruption throughout the country end. Grant us courage to be compassionate and to stand in solidarity with all who suffer from unjust and oppressive conditions. Amen.

Facilitator: Prepare group for viewing the DVD "When Freedom?/Sudan in Captivity."

Group Activity #1: The Politics of War (30 minutes)
Facilitator: Divide the class into four smaller groups and assign each group one of the possible causes of the military conflict in Darfur.
- Global Climate Changes
- Failed Counterinsurgency
- Ethnic Cleansing
- Colonial Occupation

Interview: "The Myth of War" with Emily Wax (15 minutes)
Facilitator: The interview with Emily Wax is printed in **Appendix G**. Introduce Emily Wax and the topic for discussion. Remind the group that they are to listen attentively to the interview and be prepared to respond to

the questions below. In groups of three or four, discuss the questions and then report back to total group.

Group Activity #2: Questions for Discussion (10 minutes)

- In September 2004, then-Secretary of State Colin Powell referred to the atrocities in Darfur as "genocide." Many world governments have drawn the line at labeling what has happened at Darfur as genocide. UMCOR has taken the position that the use of the word genocide heightens the danger to its aid workers in the region. Some have called the conflict a case of ethnic cleansing, and others have described it as a government going too far in trying to put down a rebellion. How would you describe the catastrophic situation in Darfur?

- The International Criminal Court's prosecutor, Luis Moreno-Ocampo, has asked for a review of evidence of genocide and crimes against humanity committed by Sudanese President Omar Hassan al-Bashir and several members of his government. Discuss your thoughts on these charges. (Reference: NPR Africa Update broadcast July 14, 2008.)

Facilitator: Summarize the key issues resulting from the wars in Sudan. (Refer to the chart you developed for this session.) Emphasize the importance of food preservation and the role women play in the production and distribution of food for their families. (This leads into Radio Interview #2.)

Listen to the Voices of Africans (15 minutes)
Radio Interview: Angelina and Jane Ohuma

Group Activity #3: Multinational Issues (20 minutes)

Facilitator: Divide the class into four small groups and assign each group one of the following issues to discuss and report back to the total class:

1. Human rights disaster
2. The grab for resources
3. The politics of oil: US policy in Sudan
4. Displacement and trafficking of persons

Facilitator: Closing comments and assignments for the next session.

Closing Hymn: "For the Healing of the Nations," *The United Methodist Hymnal, #428*

Assignment for Session 4:

- Read Chapters Four and Five in the textbook.
- Ask six volunteers to make a 10-minute report outlining the major features of the following models for peace in Sudan:

1. Models from African Americans and models of African Origin
2. The Sharia Model
3. The Humanitarian and Partnership Models
4. The "Africans for Africa" Model
5. The International Model
6. The Church's Moral Authority and Sudan's Dream of Peace

- Ask 4 volunteers to review and report on the 2008 General Conference Resolution on Sudan: A Call to Compassion and Caring. (See Chapter Five, pages 72-76.) At the end of the report, give each member of the class a 3" x 5" index card and ask them to write down one thing they will do as an outcome of the study to help bring peace to Sudan. The four volunteers will collect the cards and prepare a resolution that the class will offer as its commitment statement during the closing worship service.

Four-Session Study
Session 4: The Dream of Peace

Objectives
- To examine the Sudan Comprehensive Peace Agreement (CPA), signed January 9, 2005.
- To explore various models for peace in Sudan.
- To learn what The United Methodist Church has done to make a difference in Sudan.
- To review and study the 2008 General Conference Resolution on Sudan: A Call to Compassion and Caring.
- To explore the "next steps," including ways The United Methodist Church can be in solidarity with the Sudanese pewople.

Required Materials and Supplies
- Bible
- *The United Methodist Hymnal, Global Praise 1*
- Newsprint, magic markers, tape
- 3" x 5" multicolored index cards
- CD player
- Computer and Internet connection, if possible
- DVD player and monitor
- Secure *"Gifts of Hope: UMCOR in Darfur,"* DVD, ©2007 General Board of Global Ministries.

Preparation and Room Set-up
- Make copies of the 2008 General Conference Resolution on Sudan for each member of the class.
- Prepare a large display of the summary of the Sudan Comprehensive Peace Agreement (CPA) signed January 9, 2005. (See **sidebar**: Comprehensive Peace Agreement Summary, Chapter Three.)
- Plan to show *"Gifts of Hope: UMCOR in Darfur,"* DVD, © 2007 General Board of Global Ministries as part of this session or during the closing Service of Commitment.

Opening Worship (15 minutes)
Hymn: "There's a Spirit in the Air" (stanzas 1-3), *The United Methodist Hymnal*, #192

Bible Study and Reflection: *Isaiah 58:6-12*

Facilitator: Ask a volunteer to read Isaiah 58:6-12 as participants follow along in their Bibles. Then read the following reflections by Dr. Silvia Regina de Lima Silva, a Brazilian theologian:

> "The words of Isaiah are directed towards those who have the power because they had the power to untie those who had been subjected. On the other hand, the prophet also makes a call for solidarity among those who are tied to the same yoke. He invites them to change everyday relations, to seek forms of life in which bread can be eaten and shared, to live together, and to cover each other, and to protect and take care of each person's body. This is a *Call to Compassion and Caring*."

In small groups, have participants discuss the following:
- How can the Christian community be in solidarity with the people of Sudan?
- How should United Methodists respond to the *"Call to Compassion and Caring"*?

Hymn: "There's a Spirit in the Air" (stanzas 4-6), *The United Methodist Hymnal*, #192

Prayer: God of mercy and power, you have charged us to pray for all governments and leaders of nations. May all in positions of authority demonstrate your vision of justice, righteousness, and mercy. Help those leaders with power overcome all forms of violence, abuse, fraud, and corruption of people and all creation, so that security, peace, and harmony may reign in Sudan and worldwide. Amen!

Reports: Models of Peace (50-60 minutes)

- Models of African Americans and Models of African Origin
- The Sharia Model
- Humanitarian and Partnership Models
- "Africans for Africa" Model
- International Model
- The Church's Moral Authority and Sudan's Dream of Peace

Group Activity #1: Signs of Hope in Sudan (15 minutes)

Facilitator: Divide the class into seven small groups and have them discuss one of the following signs of hope for peace in Sudan. Have the group appoint a recorder to report key discussion points to total group. Use newsprint for the reports.

Group 1: How United Methodists Have Already Made a Difference.

Group 2: General Conference Resolution on Sudan: A Call to Compassion and Caring (Pre-assigned to four volunteers).

Group 3: Sudan Comprehensive Peace Agreement (CPA) signed January 9, 2005.

Group 4: International Criminal Court Role.

Group 5: How Sudanese Women are Modeling Peace.

Group 6: How the Global Church is Fostering Peace in Sudan.

Group 7: Implementing a Culture of Accountability.

Report: "Seven Steps for Peace in Darfur" (10 minutes)

Facilitator: *THE NEXT STEPS!*

The mission study resource on Sudan ends here, but the story of Sudan and its dream of peace and justice have not yet found their resolution. Sudan still bleeds and its troubles seem so far away. The story of Sudan has not been among the top stories in today's news media. At times, it must appear to the Sudanese people that their story has been ignored by the world community. But our faith assures us that God has not abandoned them or their rich culture that has survived and thrived for many centuries.

The Sudanese poet, Al-Saddiq Al-Raddi, suggests in his lyric poem, "A Monkey at the Window," how the stirrings of liberty, leadership, and peace stay alive in Sudan. He uses the symbol of a small, playful child to affirm that the spirit of the Sudanese people is strong. He affirms that the people will "paint things awake," will transcend their varied and conflicting tribal heritages, the oppression of colonial times, and today's crushing issues, to realize the birth of a strong, viable nation.

> The solid front door remembers the hand that
> made it. You are the key—
> and the creak of the universe—it's your sole
> secret.
> You lean your dreams and future against it.
> For its sake you endure the woodworms
> gnawing thought your heart, the reek of damp,
> the hammering of enemies and relatives.

(Long is the absence of light
That paints things awake –
Long is the presence of paint.)

Service of Commitment: Signs of Hope (20 minutes)

Leader: Hear the word of God, as it is recorded in Acts 1:8. "But you will receive power when the Holy Spirit has come upon you; and you will be my witnesses in Jerusalem, in all Judea and Samaria, and to the ends of the earth."

All: Lord, inspire your church to be a witness of your love, compassion, and healing in a world that is hurting and desperate for the good news of hope, liberation, and peace.

Leader: We have listened to the stories of our brothers and sisters in Sudan, and we have heard their moaning and their cries for help.

All: Lord, send out your church to lift up those who suffer and carry heavy burdens due to situations beyond their control.

Leader: O God of the nations, comfort those who have lost loved ones in ongoing wars, droughts, floods, earthquakes, hurricanes.

All: Inspire hope in the devastating chaos in the world. Empower your church to join together to help restore peace and harmony in Sudan and throughout the world.

UMCOR, "Gifts of Hope: UMCOR in Darfur," DVD, 2007 General Board of Global Ministries

Signs of Commitment: Have the class resolution presented at this time. Then invite all members of the class to come forward, light the candle they were given, and return to their seats as the group sings, "Siyahamba" ("We Are Marching in the Light of God"), *The Faith We Sing*, p. 2235b.

Leader: Go in peace and may the peace of God go with you. Amen!

Appendices

Appendix A
A Chronology of Key Events in Sudan

Pre-19th Century

- From remote antiquity until recent times the northern portion of the territory comprising modern Sudan formed part of the region known as Nubia. The history of Nilotic, or Southern Sudan before the 19th century is obscure. Many of the oral and written histories have disappeared, lost to the destructive attitudes of colonialism and the hardships of war. We do know that during the period of the Old Kingdom (about 2575-2134 BCE), Egyptian penetration of Nubia began. By 1500 BCE, when the 18th dynasty was founded, Nubia had been reduced to the status of an Egyptian province.

- Egyptian dominance ended with a Nubian revolt in the 8th century BCE. A succession of independent kingdoms was subsequently established in Nubia. The most powerful of these, Makuria, a Christian state centered at Old Dunquiah and founded in the 6th century AD, endured until the early 14th century invasion of the Egyptian Mamluka. Around 1500, the Funj, black Muslims of uncertain origin, overwhelmed Alwa in the vicinity of present-day Khartoum, establishing a sultanate at Sennar.

- During the 16th century, the Funj emerged as a powerful Islamic state, and Sennar became one of the great cultural centers of Islam. Dissension among the leading Funj tribes vastly weakened the kingdom during the final years of the 18th century. In 1820 it was invaded by an Egyptian army. The ensuing war ended in 1822 with a complete victory for Egypt.

19th Century

1820-1880: Egypt conquers northern parts of Sudan, developing ivory and slave trades.

1881-1889: Nationalist revolts, led by Muhammed Ahmad Al Mahdi, begin to form in opposition to Egyptian and British rule. The British and Egyptians are defeated in 1885 and Al Mahdi establishes a theocracy in Khartoum.

1890-1899: Britain regains control of Sudan with military campaigns led by Lord Kitchener. In 1899, Egypt and Britain agree on joint government of Sudan.

20th Century

1930-1946: The British Civil Secretary in Khartoum declared the "Southern Policy," officially stating what had always been in practice: the North and South, because of their many cultural and religious differences, are governed as two separate regions.

1946-1955: Britain and Khartoum (by this time Egypt is effectively out of the picture) abruptly decided to merge North and South into a single administrative region. Arabic is made the language of administration in the South, and Northerners begin to hold positions there.

1955: First Sudanese Civil War begins.

1956: On January 1, 1956, independence is granted to Sudan as a single unified nation.

First Sudanese Civil War Period, 1955–1972

1958: General Ibrahim Abbud leads military coup against the civilian government elected earlier in the year.

1962: Civil war spreads to Southern Sudan led by the Anyanya separatist movement.

1964: The "October Revolution" overthrows Abbud's regime and a national government is established.

1969: Gaafar al-Nimerei leads the "May Revolution" military coup.

1971: Attempted Communist coup against Nimeiri fails and the leaders are executed.

1972: The Addis Ababa peace agreement between the Sudanese government and the Anyanya create a self-governing region in the South.

1978: Oil discovered in Bentiu in Southern Sudan.

Second Sudanese Civil War Period 1983–2005

1983:
- Civil war breaks out again in the South involving government forces and the Sudan People's Liberation Movement (SPLM), led by John Garang.
- President Nimeiri declares the introduction of Sharia (Islamic law).
- Civil war pitted Muslim North against Christian and animist South.

1985: After widespread popular unrest Nimeiri is deposed by a group of officers and a Transitional Military Council is set up to rule the country.

1986: Sadiq al-Mahdi becomes prime minister.

Various peace negotiation attempts between al-Mahdi and the Sudan People's Liberation Movement (SPLM) fail as the conflict worsens.

1989: As al-Mahdi moved toward signing certain peace agreements, he was ousted in a coup and on June 30, Omar al-Bashir seized power and assumes the office of president.

1993: On October 16, 1993, Omar al-Bashir is appointed president. He is supported by the fundamentalist National Islamic Front (NIF) and the new government fiercely enforces Islamic code throughout Sudan.

United States Strike

1995: Egyptian President Hosni Mubarak accuses Sudan of being involved in attempts to assassinate him in Addis Ababa.

1998:
- After embassy bombings in Kenya and Tanzania, the United States launched a missile attack on a pharmaceutical factory outside Khartoum, alleging that it was producing chemical weapons for terrorist groups.
- New constitution endorsed by over 96 percent of voters in referendum.

1999:
- President Bashir dissolves the National Assembly and declares a state of emergency following a power struggle with parliamentary speaker, Hassan al-Turabi.
- Almost 4,000 Sudanese refugee boys are approved for resettlement to the United States.
- Sudan begins to export oil.

2000:
- The Governor of Khartoum bans women working in public places.

- President Bashir meets leaders of opposition National Democratic Alliance for the first time in Eritrea.
- Main opposition parties boycott presidential elections. Incumbent Bashir is reelected for a five-year term as president.

21st Century
2001:

- Famine affects three million Sudanese. United Nations World Food Programme struggles to feed the millions facing starvation.
- Islamist leader Hassan al-Turabi's party, the Popular National Congress, signs memorandum of understanding with the southern rebel SPLM's armed wing, the Sudan People's Liberation Army (SPLA). Al-Turabi is arrested the next day, with more arrests of PNC members in the following months.
- SPLA threatens to attack foreign oil workers.
- Peace talks in Nairobi break down.
- Egypt and Libya propose a peace plan for Sudan.
- UN lifts sanctions against Sudan.
- President George W. Bush appoints former US Senator John Danforth as the President's Special Envoy for Peace in Sudan.
- US extends unilateral sanctions against Sudan for another year, citing its record on terrorism and rights violations.

Peace Deals
2002:

- Government and SPLA sign landmark ceasefire agreement providing for six-month renewable ceasefire in central Nuba Mountains, a key rebel stronghold.
- Talks in Kenya lead to a breakthrough agreement between the government and southern rebels on ending the 19-year civil war. The Machakos Protocol provides for the South to seek self-determination after six years.

2003:

- Rebels in western region of Darfur rise up against government, claiming the region is being neglected by Khartoum.
- PNC leader Turabi released after nearly three years in detention and ban on the party lifted.

Uprising in West
2004:

- Army moves to quell rebel uprising in western region of Darfur; hundreds of thousands of refugees flee to neighboring Chad. Darfur conflict has killed tens of thousands, and displaced millions.
- UN official says pro-government Arab *janjaweed* militias are carrying out systematic killings of African villagers in Darfur.
- US Secretary of State Colin Powell describes Darfur killings as genocide.

Peace Agreement
2005:

- **9 January** - Comprehensive Peace Agreement between the SPLA and the government signed. The agreement includes a permanent ceasefire and accords on wealth- and power-sharing.
- **March** - UN Security Council authorizes sanctions against those who violate the

Darfur ceasefire. Council also votes to refer those accused of war crimes in Darfur to International Criminal Court.

- **June** - Islamist leader Hassan al-Turabi is freed after being detained since March 2004.

Southern Autonomy
2005:

- **9 July** - Former southern rebel leader John Garang is sworn in as first vice president. A constitution which gives a large degree of autonomy to the South is signed.
- **1 August** - John Garang killed in a plane crash; he is succeeded by Salva Kiir. Garang's death sparks deadly clashes in the capital between Southern Sudanese and Northern Arabs.
- **September** - A power-sharing government is established in Khartoum.
- **October** - Autonomous government is formed in the South, in line with January 2005 peace deal. The administration is dominated by former rebels.

Darfur Conflict
2006:

- **May** - Khartoum government and the main rebel faction in Darfur, the Sudan Liberation Movement, sign a peace accord. Two smaller rebel groups reject the deal. Fighting continues.
- **August** - Sudan rejects a UN resolution calling for a UN peacekeeping force in Darfur for six months.
- **October** - Jan Pronk, head of the United Nations Mission in Sudan, expelled from the country.

- **November** - African Union extends mandate of its peacekeeping force in Darfur for further six months.

2007:

- April - Sudan says it will accept a partial UN troop deployment to reinforce African Union peacekeeping in Darfur, but not a full 20,000-strong force.
- May - International Criminal Court issues arrest warrants for a minister and a *janjaweed* militia leader suspected of Darfur war crimes.
- May - US President George W. Bush places fresh sanctions on Sudan.
- 31 July - UN Security Council Resolution 1769 authorizes 26,000 peacekeepers for Darfur. Sudan says it will cooperate with the UN-African Union Mission in Darfur (UNAMID).
- August-September - 2007 Sudan floods.
- October - SPLM temporarily suspends participation in national unity government, accusing Khartoum of failing to honor the 2005 peace deal.
- December - SPLM resumes participation in national unity government.

2008:

- **January** - UN takes over Darfur peace force.
- Within days Sudan apologizes after its troops fire on a convoy of UNAMID, the UN-African Union hybrid mission.
- Government planes bomb rebel positions in West Darfur, turning some areas into no-go zones for aid workers.
- **February** - Commander of the UN-African Union peacekeepers in Darfur, Balla Keita, says more troops needed urgently in West Darfur.

- **March** - Russia says it is prepared to provide some of the helicopters urgently needed by UN-African Union peacekeepers.
- Tensions rise over clashes between an Arab militia and SPLM in Abyei area on North-South divide; a key sticking point in 2005 peace accord.
- Presidents of Sudan and Chad sign accord aimed at halting five years of hostilities between their countries.
- **April** - Counting begins in national census which is seen as a vital step towards holding democratic elections after the landmark 2005 North-South peace deal. The 2008 census count could have a big impact on Sudan's political future.
- UN humanitarian chief John Holmes says 300,000 people may have died in the five-year Darfur conflict.
- **May** - Southern defense minister Dominic Dim Deng is killed in a plane crash in the South.
- Tension increases between Sudan and Chad after Darfur rebel group mounts raid on Omdurman, Khartoum's twin city across the Nile. Sudan accuses Chad of involvement and breaks off diplomatic relations.
- Intense fighting breaks out between Northern and Southern forces in disputed oil-rich town of Abyei.
- **June** - President al-Bashir and southern leader Salva Kiir agree to seek international arbitration to resolve dispute over Abyei.

(Source: "Timeline: Sudan, BBC News". Retrieved on 2007-12-02)

A man writes out portions of the Koran in the Dereig Camp for internally displaced persons.
(Paul Jeffrey, ACT-Caritas)

Appendix B
Sudan Facts Match Game

Directions: Match the phases, numbers, or statements in Column A with the correct response in Column B.

COLUMN A	COLUMN B
1. Land area North and South	a. Approximate population of Darfur
2. Women over age 65	b. Number of women over age 15 who can read and write
3. Agriculture	c. 4.7 million
4. Size of Texas	d. 40,218,455
5. 5,932,344	e. Men over age 65
6. Fifty years	f. ¼ the size of the USA
7. Population North and South	g. Main occupation
8. 518,822	h. 18.9 years
9. Official language	i. Major religions of Sudan
10. Cell phones in use	j. Darfur
11. 7,400,000	k. Capital of Sudan
12. Median age	l. Life expectancy
13. Muslims, Christians, traditional beliefs	m. 471, 530
14. 540	n. Seventy percent
15. Sunni Muslims	o. Number of diverse languages
16. Khartoum	p. Arabic

Appendix C
Sudan Facts & Figures

BASIC FACTS	
Official name	Republic of the Sudan
Capital	Khartoum
Area	2,505,800 sq. km. (967,490 sq. ml.)
PEOPLE	
Population	40,000,000
Population growth Population growth rate	2.64 percent (2004 estimate)
Projected population by 2025	61, 338,891 (2004 estimate)
Projected population by 2050	84,192,309 (2004 estimate)
Population Density	17 persons per sq. km. (2004 estimate) 43 persons per sq. ml. (2004 estimate)
Urban/rural distribution	
Share urban	38 percent (2002 estimate)
Share rural	62 percent (2002 estimate)
Largest cities, with population	
Khartoum	2,731,000 (2000 estimate)
Omdurman	1,267,077 (1993)
Port Sudan	505,385 (1993)
Kassala	234,270 (1993)
Nyala	228,778 (1993)
Ethnic groups	
Black African (Dinka, Nuer, Shilluk, Azande, Kakwa)	49 percent
Arab	39 percent
Nubian	8 percent
Beja	3 percent
Other	1 percent
Languages	
Arabic (official), Nubian, Dinka, Nuer, Bari, Lotuko, English	

Religious affiliations	
Sunni Muslim (in the North)	70 percent
Ethnoreligionist or indigenous beliefs	12 percent
Christian* (mostly in the South and Khartoum)	15 percent
Other	3 percent
HEATH AND EDUCATION	
Life expectancy	
Total**	58.1 years (2004 estimate)
Female	59.4 years (2004 estimate)
Male	57 years (2004 estimate)
Literacy Rate	
Total	62.2 percent (2004 estimate)
Female	51.9 percent (2004 estimate)
Male	72.6 percent (2004 estimate)
Number of years of compulsory schooling	8 years (2000)
Number of students per teacher, primary school	27 students per teacher (1999-2000)

* Note: This percentage differs from the figure given on page 15 of the adult study guide. The number of Christians in Sudan is uncertain, and sources are often contradictory.

** Note: Again, this figure differs from the age given in the adult study guide.

(Source: Microsoft Encarta Encyclopedia *2005)*

Appendix D
Voices from Sudan: WSCM Radio Africa Interviews

[This is a simulated interview, adapted from articles in the adult study, and is meant solely for class re-enactment.]

Interview #1: Saba and Musayahia

Reporter: Good afternoon! Welcome to WSCM RADIO AFRICA broadcast program. This week our focus is on Sudan, and the escalating crisis in Darfur that has claimed the lives of more than 300,000 and displaced two million to four million persons. This is the first in a series of interviews with displaced Sudanese who were fortunate to escape their villages and resettle in Khartoum, the capital of Sudan. Our guests today, are Saba and Musayahia. Saba comes from the rural village of Zalingei in West Darfur. She, like many other villagers, fled from her home during the insurgence of militia troops in 2005.

Musayahia, is a student in Khartoum. He fled his village in 2003 after militias attacked his village. We will hear from Saba first, as she tells us what life was like before the gunmen invaded her village. Please welcome Saba and Musayahia. (Applause)

Saba: Thank you for inviting me here today. My family and I come from a rural village in West Darfur. My father was a traditional farmer in Zalingei. He raised goats and cows, not for the market but to meet family needs. But one day, men on horseback plundered our village, shooting up the land and killing some of the villagers. Some members of my family and I fled eastward on foot, and by lorry when we were lucky.

Reporter: How did you find your way to Khartoum?

Saba: My three sons, two brothers, and I traveled nearly a thousand miles by motor truck. It was a difficult and dangerous journey. We managed to avoid bandits traveling along the treacherous roads. Our old truck broke down often, but my brothers were able to fix it and keep us moving. It was a very difficult trip.

Reporter: You mentioned that your three sons were traveling with you. How old were they?

Saba: My youngest son was two and my oldest son was seven. It was hard on them, but we survived and now we are safe here in Camp Mayo.

Reporter: The camp in Mayo is one of six camps for displaced persons located in Khartoum. Would you tell us what it is like living in the camp?

Saba: There are some 250,000 displaced persons living in these camps. Jobs are hard to find. I go door-to-door looking for work. I have been able to earn a few dinar to help support my family by working as a domestic and laundry worker.

Reporter: How did you learn about UMCOR operations in Khartoum?

Saba: A member of my extended family introduced me to UMCOR. They have implemented agricultural programs in South

Darfur, helping people like my parents to regain their self-sufficiency.

Reporter: Where are your parents now?

Saba: When my brothers and I fled our village, my four sisters stayed behind to care for our parents. Not much remains of the old ways. The animals were stolen or run off by the gunmen, wells were polluted, houses burned, and people killed.

Reporter: Thank you, Saba, for sharing your story with us.

Reporter: Musayahia! Thank you for accepting our invitation to share with us your amazing story.

Musayahia: It is good to be here. I have been living in Mamora, a section of Khartoum away from the camps. I built a small dwelling where my wife, son, and father live. It's expensive to live in Khartoum, but safe. I am in school in Khartoum, studying science, math, Arabic, English, geography, and history. I want to improve my life and to find a suitable job

Reporter: When did you leave your home in Darfur?

Musayahia: I, along with seventeen others, left our village in 2003. We traveled some 700 miles by lorry. Like many others, I was forced to leave after militias attacked my village. It was rainy season, and the roads were often washed out. We watched over one another, sleeping in shifts in the open so someone was always awake to alert the others of any danger or suspicious sounds. We slept at night and traveled only during the daylight hours. It took us 15 days to travel the 700 miles.

Reporter: Do you still have family back home in Darfur?

Musayahia: Yes. My mother and a sister are living in Darfur. I send them money when I can. I hope the peace agreement signed a few months ago, will mean peace for Darfur as well. Though I lost my house and had to separate my family, I long to return home.

Reporter: We thank you both for sharing your stories with us. We hope that our audience will join other international efforts to bring a halt to the fighting and a permanent peace agreement to end the division between North and South Sudan. Please know that we, too, share your dreams and hopes of someday returning to your ancestral homes and reuniting with family and friends. This is (name) wishing you good day from WSCM RADIO AFRICA, broadcasting from Khartoum, Sudan.

Interview #2: Jane Ohuma and Angelina from the Julha Farm

Reporter: Good morning! Welcome to the second in a series of interviews conducted and sponsored by WSCM RADIO AFRICA.

We are broadcasting today's program from the Julha Farm, a women's farm in Ed Daein, South Darfur. Here to tell us more about Julha is Jane Ohuma, United Methodist Committee on Relief's (UMCOR) head of mission and Angelina, one of a dozen or so women who help cultivate this land. Please welcome our guests.

Reporter: I'd like to start with Angelina. Angelina, tell us how you came to be part of this community.

Angelina: I had to flee my home state of Bar Al Gazahl just south of Julha Farm. Armed militia raided our village, murdering relatives, destroying cattle and crops, and I fled for fear of being raped, killed, or sold into slavery.

Reporter: What is life like for you here at Julha Farm?

Angelina: The work is hard but very satisfying. I work from sunup to sundown with my child wrapped on my back in a sling. The crops we raise feed our families and provide income for cash crops we sell.

Reporter: Thank you Angelina for sharing your story. Now, Jane, will you tell us more about Julha Farm and how United Methodist Committee on Relief is involved?

Jane: First, I want to express my appreciation for this opportunity to be on this show. Julha is a farm located in Ed Daein, near El Ferdous, a community of displaced Darfurians. The land is cultivated by a dozen women, Angelina among them, who work tirelessly every day of the week. UMCOR provides seeds and containers for the women to carry water. UMCOR also provides training for these women, teaching them to be self-sufficient.

Reporter: Does UMCOR sponsor other farms like Julha?

Jane: With a grant from a remarkable congregation, the Ginghamsburg United Methodist Church in Ohio, UMCOR started a seeds and tools program in several communities in South Darfur. In August 2005 some 5,200 families had crops under cultivation. The number today has reached over 10,000.

I believe that teaching women to be self-sufficient is a first step in helping a community to recover after decades of instability. Women can influence the nutrition of entire families, for example. When they gain the confidence of learning new farming skills, they transmit that confidence, the skills, and even extra income to their families. In a culture where the life of a woman is undervalued, these are important strides forward.

Reporter: How much land does each head of household receive and what crops are grown?

Jane: Each head of household at Julha received two measures of millet to plant in the sandy soil and one measure of sorghum to plant in clay. With the aid of UM-COR agronomist, Abdul Rahim Malik, the women were taught to intercrop, or mingle these plantings with other seeds such as groundnuts and beans. Okra and melon seeds are interplanted as cash crops. All of these crops are being cultivated by a half dozen families, all of whom are headed by women.

Reporter: What an exciting program! Angelina, you must feel very good about the contributions you and the other women are making to the rebuilding of your region.

Angelina: Oh, yes, I do! However, I long to return to my home. I left when I was quite young and I miss the people I left behind. It would be great to see them.

Reporter: Angelina and Jane, thank you both for sharing your stories with us today. You have helped us understand and identify some of the issues involved in the confrontations in South Sudan. We support your efforts and join you in prayer for a speedy end to the war in Darfur. This is (name) wishing you good day from **WSCM RADIO AFRICA,** broadcasting from South Darfur, Sudan.

Appendix E
The People of Sudan

Arabs

Around 40 percent of the population identify themselves as Arab and speak Arabic as mother tongue. The term Arab refers to tribes descended from a common ancestor. However, the label is as much cultural as it is lineal.

There are two main Arab tribes in Sudan, namely the **Jaalayin**, and **Juhayna**. The Jaalayin are agriculturalists mainly living along the Nile, from Dongola to south of Khartoum. The Juhayna have two main divisions: the Kabbabish are camel herders in the West, while the Baggara Arabs are found mainly in southern Kordofan and Darfur, raising cattle along the borders with the non-Muslim area of Southern Sudan.

Beja

The second largest Muslim group is the **Beja**, semi-nomads who live along the Red Sea coast and from Kassala to the Arbara River. An ancient people known to the Romans, the Beja adopted Islam early. They are traditionally herders of camels and sheep. Due to drought, many have taken up agriculture. They are famed warriors and suspicious of most forms of governments.

Nuba

The **Nubians** are the third most populous Muslim people in Sudan. They live along the Nile, around the Third Cataract and up into southern Egypt. They have their own language and a strong cultural identity dating back to their pre-Islamic Christian and Kushite heritage. Due to the construction of Aswan Dam in the 1960s and the flooding of much of their homeland, thousands of Nubians were forced to resettle on the Arbara River near Kassala. Today, there are as many Nubians living in Khartoum as in Nubia itself.

Other Muslim Peoples

The **Fellata** are descended from West Africa migrants, mostly Hausa and Fulani, who traveled through the country en route to Mecca. They were encouraged to settle and farm in Sudan.

Around a million Fellata live in Sudan with many settled in the rich agricultural area of Gezira.

In Darfur, the dominant ethnic groups are the **Fur** and **Massalit**. Both tribes are black African farmers. The Fur are the old rulers of Darfur's sultanate and were known for their skill with horses. They controlled the trading and economic center for the mountainous western region known as Jebbal Marra. Late in the 16th century an Islamic sultanate took over, and the Fur adopted Arabic language, the religious practices, and dress. Today they are entirely Muslim, though are considered "non-Arab," because even with intermarriage their heritage is that of indigenous people of the region. Land is the maker of wealth, and the very wealthy few practice polygyny, the marriage of a man to more than one woman.

The **Massalit** and the **Zaghawa** tribes are non-Arab groups living north of the Fur in the border area of Chad. Living as neighbors are an Arab group, the *Baqqarah* (an Arab word meaning "cattle herders") who are descendents of Egyptian Arabs. The *Baqqarah* (also spelled *Baggarah*) probably migrated into Darfur and other northern regions during the 18th century. The Fur and Massalit have both have been targets of the insurgency in Darfur since 2003.

Dinka

The **Dinka** are the largest non-Arab ethnic group in Southern Sudan, numbering some 4 million. One tenth of the Dinka population speak Dinka as a first language.

They count their wealth in cattle which are central to their culture. As pastoral people the Dinka, called *Jieng* in their own language, migrate regularly as do their Nuer neighbors, cultivating crops during the rainy seasons in villages built on high ground, and sheltering and feeding their cattle in the riverine pasture lands in dry season. Cattle are also sacrificed in Dinka religious ceremonies. Non-Christian and non-Muslim Dinka worship the life-giving god, Nhial, whom they can contact through intermediaries in rituals conducted by tribal members who have the gifts of healing and divination. Ancestors are also believed to be sources of strength in everyday life.

The Dinka dominate the Sudanese People's Liberation Movement Army (SPLM/A).

Nuer

The **Nuer** live in clusters of communities along the banks of the Nile River. Primarily cattle farmers, they supplement their diets with millet and fish. They split their time between riverside settlements in dry season, and higher-ground villages in flood season. Traditional Nuer families are polygynous. Religious worship among Nuers who did not convert to Christianity honors a single creator thought to be all-surrounding but also to take form in some plants and animals. Nuers and Dinkas are traditional rivals.

Misseriya

The **Misseriya**, traditionally known as Arabs, are the neighbors of the Dinka and Nuer. They were among the migrants into Sudan from the East in the 18th century and brought to the region the practice of moving their cattle between pasturelands in the South and the North in response to seasonal changes. Tension between the Dinka and Misseriya over grazing rights, power-sharing, and other political and economic considerations are not new. On April 15, 2007, Dinka and Misseriya traders signed an agreement that formed the "Abyei Chamber of Commerce: the Union of Dinka and Misseriya Traders."

Shilluk

The **Shilluk**, together with their White Nile neighbors, the Nuer and Dinka, make up about 20 percent of Sudan's total population. Related by language to the others, the Shilluk hunt, fish, herd cattle and goats, and grow staple grains such as millet in their settlements along the west banks. This sedentary lifestyle has led to permanent settlements and a centralized political economy far removed from the loose tribal structure of the Nuer and Dinka. Like the Nuer, the Shilluk are monotheistic, with the belief that the creative force is symbolized in real life by certain plants, animals, and signs.

Equatorians

The **Azande**, living in the southern quarter of the country, are the largest Equatorian tribe in Sudan. Their language belongs to the Niger-Congo family. They are an agricultural, hierarchical society, headed by a king. They were the first to take advantage of British education policies, and were early supporters of the Anyanya rebels in the first civil war.

Smaller Equatorian tribes include the **Bari** and **Mandari**, who live around Juba.

Reference: Sudan, The Bradt Travel Guide, by Paul Clammer, The Globe Pequot Press Inc., USA, Reprint 2007.

Appendix F
Religion in Sudan

Islam

Sunni Islam is one of the two main branches of Islam. Shia Islam is the other. Sunni Muslims constitute the vast majority of Muslims in the world Islamic community and account for around 70 percent of Muslims in Sudan. The term *sunna* means the "way" or the "example" and refers to the example of the Prophet Muhammad. All Islamic groups and sects, however, accept the *sunna*, along with the Qur'an, the sacred scriptures of Islam, as binding.

The two main branches of Islam differ primarily in their beliefs about the succession to Muhammad. Sunni Muslims believe that Muhammad intended that the Muslim community choose a successor, or caliph, by consensus to lead the theocracy (earthly kingdom under divine rule) he had set up. Shia Muslims, also known as Shias, believe that Muhammad chose his son-in-law, Ali, as his successor, and that only the descendents of Ali and his wife, Fatima, were entitled to rule the Muslim community. There are also differences between the two branches in interpretation of the Qur'an.

Islam first arrived in Sudan with the Arabs as part of their expansion following the death of the Prophet Muhammad in the 7th century AD. Islamization was a slow process as the Arabs initially kept to their nomadic traditions, instead of creating new political structures as they took control of the land.

The rise of the Funj Kingdom at the start of the 16th century paved the way for the great spread of Islam across Sudan. While Islam took hold in the North of Sudan from Darfur to the Red Sea, the South remained a barrier to the Arabs. The Sudd proved impenetrable, and it wasn't until the mid-19th century that Arab traders entered the region in any numbers. British policies during the Condominium explicitly prevented the spread of Islam into the South by restricting the movement of Arab and other northern traders in the region. Following independence these restraints were removed.

Islamization is a major source of conflict between the North and South. Nimeiri's declaration of sharia across the South was the spark that re-lit the war in 1983; President Bashir later called for a *jihad* (holy struggle) against the Southern rebels. Elsewhere, the Nuba have found that their lack of Muslim credentials has led to the confiscation and gift of their fertile agricultural land to Arab farmers. In contemporary Sudan, Islam is as much a political issue as a religion.

Christianity

In contrast to the Northern states in Sudan, which are predominately Muslim, Southern Sudan is often called "the Christian South" in Western media. Sudan is home to some two million Christians, and almost all of them live in the South.

Coptic Christians from Egypt arrived in Sudan during the 4th century and Melkite missionaries in 543. Byzantine missionaries brought Christianity to Sudan in the 5th century AD. The Christian kingdom of Nubia prospered for 600 years before giving way to Islam in the 14th century. Modern Sudanese Christians, who make up 5 percent of the population, are the product of Western missionary enterprises starting in the mid-19th century.

Under British rule, missionaries were encouraged to operate in Southern Sudan. The South was divided into spheres of influence for the many Christian sects, who were allowed to open schools and churches. The mission had a larger impact on education than on rates of conversion to Christianity.

One of the most enduring of the Christian missions was that of the Catholic Verona Fathers, who first came to Sudan in 1854. Their head, Daniel Comboni, became the first Bishop of Central Africa. He died in Khartoum and was canonized 100 years later for his work. Roman Catholic missionaries arrived in 1861, although their mission was largely destroyed during an insurrection in 1881. The Roman Catholic Church was reestablished in 1898, and the Anglicans followed in 1899.

The Anglicans pioneered girls' schools in both North and South. Today, the Roman Catholic and Anglican churches are the largest denominations in Sudan. There are also Coptic, Ethiopian, Greek Orthodox, and United Methodist churches.

Outwardly, Christianity appears to be in good health in Sudan. Churches are common and the Christian holy days are observed as public holidays. While ground-level relations between Christians and Muslims are generally good, the Islamic policies of successive governments tell a different story.

The Foreign Missionary Act passed in 1962 classified churches as foreign institutions rather than domestic ones, and has repeatedly been used to confiscate church land. Muslims converted to Christianity face the death penalty and priests and congregations alike are subject to harassment. The Sudanese Council of Churches and the Sudan Catholic Bishops' Conference have repeatedly spoken out against the discrimination against Christians. The status of Sudanese Christians has found resonance with evangelical lobbying groups in the US and influenced the policies of the government. Despite the Islamic policies of recent years, conversions to Christianity have increased faster in this period than during the nearly 60 years of British rule.

Traditional Religions

A fifth of the Sudanese population subscribe to traditional African religions, overwhelmingly in the Nilotic South. These are often lumped together under the unhelpful umbrella of animism, a term that says more about Western prejudices than about any religious practices actually found in Sudan. Animism indicates a worldview dominated by supernatural and primal spirits that order the world, and the worship of those spirits. The truth is that the ethnic groups in the South have highly developed theistic beliefs.

While religions vary, there is an almost universal belief in a supreme creator or God, who is omnipotent, timeless, and remote from man. Concepts of an afterlife are less common; a more typical belief is that the world is divided into visible and invisible realms. The latter are populated by spirits, with those of ancestors often playing an important role in day-to-day life. Spirits are aspects of God and are used to explain the workings of the world rather than to directly alter it.

Worship of the Supreme Being is most developed among the Shilluk, the Dinka, and the Nuer. The Nuer have no single word for the concept of God. The creator is often referred to as Kwoth. In the face of their creator, the Nuer consider themselves ants, and the bridge between the earth and the sky (where God is found) is too great to cross. Instead, God is manifested through spirits. Spirits of the sun, rain, and of the Nuer's ancestors are particularly important. There is no belief in an afterlife. The Nuer use sacrifice as a central part of their relationship with God in rites of passage ceremonies and as appeasement for acts within the community. Cattle, being highly prized, are used in sacrifices.

For the Dinka, the supreme creator is Jok, also a collective name for ancestral spirits. Nyikang, the god of the Shilluk, is both the universal spirit and the founding ancestor of the people. All Shilluk kings are the direct descendants of Nyikang and his incarnations.

Reference: Sudan, The Bradt Travel Guide, by Paul Clammer, The Globe Pequot Press, Inc., USA, Reprint 2007.

Appendix G
Interview with Emily Wax: The Myths of War

[This is a simulated interview, adapted from articles in the adult study, and is meant solely for class re-enactment.]

Facilitator: I am pleased to introduce Emily Wax, writer for *The Washington Post* and its East Africa bureau chief. Her article, "Five Truths About Darfur," appeared in the April 23, 2006 edition of *The Washington Post*. She has traveled extensively through Africa and to the Darfur region.

Emily has graciously agreed to share with us some of her views on the issues fueling the war in Darfur. Please welcome Emily Wax to our class. (Applause)

Facilitator: As you know, some media analyses have created a narrative that tells only a partial story about the war in Darfur. Some claim that this is a religious war between Muslims and Christians. Others suggest that the conflict is between Arabs and Black Africans. Oversimplification of the causes of the conflict has stemmed in part from cultural misunderstanding and prejudices. But there are other factors to be considered. In your April 2006 article, "Five Truths about Darfur," you set forth several myths about the war in Darfur. What are your viewpoints on the war?

Emily Wax: In my travels, I've seen destroyed mosques all over Darfur. The few men left in the villages shared the same story: As government Antonov jets dropped bombs, *janjaweed* militia members rode in on horseback and attacked the town's mosque—usually the largest structure in town. The strange thing they said was that the attackers were Muslim, too. Darfur is home to some of Sudan's most devout Muslims, in a country where 65 percent of the population practices Islam, the official state religion. The long-running war between Sudan's North and South did have religious undertones mixed with the drive on the part of the South to share in the governance of Sudan. However, the war in Darfur is different. Darfur is about resources and who controls them. We are talking about land, water, access to economic development and livelihoods, and connection to political influence. The war is about the grab of resources by the most powerful from the least.

Facilitator: Another reason often cited for the cause of the conflict in Darfur is that the war is between Arabs and Black Africans. How do you respond to these analysts?

Emily Wax: Although the conflict has been framed as a battle between Arabs and black Africans, everyone in Darfur appears to be dark-skinned, at least by the usual Western standards. Sudan melds African and Arab identities. Especially in Darfur, these groups have been integrated through intermarriage, bloodlines, and cultural assimilation for generations. The true division in Darfur is between ethnic groups, split between herders and farmers. Two decades of scarcity and famine have spurred this conflict between groups of tribes whose main economic advantage are their animals and groups whose economies are based on farming. As Arabs began to dominate the centers of government and laws in the past century, it became politically expedient for people to call themselves Arab, no matter what their tribal identity. All sides, however, have engaged in atrocities heightened by ethnic slurs.

Facilitator: What role do you feel politics plays in the war in Darfur?

Emily Wax: Although the analysts have emphasized the racial and ethnic aspects of the conflict in Darfur, a long-running political battle between Sudanese President Omar Hassan al-Bashir and radical Islamic cleric Hassan al-Turabi may be more relevant.

A charismatic college professor and former speaker of parliament, Turabi has long been one of Bashir's main political rivals and an influential figure in Sudan. He has been fingered as an extremist. (As a side note, before the September 11, 2001 attacks in the US, Turabi often referred to Osama bin Laden as a hero.) More recently, the United Nations and human rights experts have accused Turabi of backing one of Darfur's key rebel groups, the Justice and Equality Movement.

Because of his clashes with Bashir, Turabi is usually under house arrest in his home in Khartoum. The rebel group, the Justice and Equality Movement, or JEM as it is known, rejected the Comprehensive Peace Agreement supported by the Bashir government because it did not ad-

dress continuing political and economic marginalization of Darfur.

In the words of Ghazi Suleiman, a Sudanese human rights lawyer, "Darfur is simply the battlefield for a power struggle over Khartoum. That's why the government hit back so hard. They saw Turabi's hand, and they want to stay in control of Sudan at any cost."

Facilitator: The war in Darfur has captured the attention of Western activists, the United Nations Security Council, the World Health Organization, and a number of nongovernmental humanitarian aid organizations, including the United Methodist Committee on Relief. These organizations are working to end the conflict and provide relief to the Sudanese people. What other roles are international entities playing in this conflict?

Emily Wax: This conflict is international. China and Chad have played key roles in the Darfur war. In 1990, Idriss Deby came to power in Chad by launching a military blitzkrieg from Darfur and overthrowing President Hissan Habre. Deby hails from the elite Zaghawa tribe, which makes up one of the Darfur rebel groups trying to topple the government. So when the conflict broke out, Deby had to decide whether to support Sudan or his tribe. He eventually chose his tribe. This allowed the Sudanese rebels to have bases in Chad. Meanwhile, Khartoum is accused of supporting Chad's anti-Deby rebels, who have a military camp in West Darfur.

Sudan is China's fourth-biggest supplier of imported oil, and that relationship carries benefits. China, which holds veto power in the UN Security Council, has said it will stand by Sudan against US efforts to slap sanctions on the country and in the battle to force Sudan to replace the African Union peacekeepers with a larger UN presence. China has built highways and factories in Khartoum, and the Friendship Conference Hall, the city's largest public meeting place.

Facilitator: Many of the world's governments have drawn the line at labeling the war in Darfur as "genocide." In your article, you state that this label has made things worse. What are your views on this war? Is this a case of "genocide," ethnic cleansing, or overaggressiveness on the part of the government?

Emily Wax: In September 2004, then Secretary of State Colin Powell referred to the conflict as a "genocide." Rather than spurring greater international action, that label seems to have strengthened Sudan's rebels; they believe they don't need to negotiate with the government and think they will have US support when they commit attacks. Peace talks have broken down seven times, partly because the rebel groups have walked out of negotiations. And Sudan's government has used the genocide label to market itself in the Middle East as another victim of America's anti-Arab and anti-Islamic policies.

Another example of the counterproductive aspect of the label is the fact that the United States has failed to follow up with any meaningful action. In late 2004, Charles Snyder, the State Department's senior representative on Sudan, told me that "the word 'genocide' was not an action word. It was a responsibility word." He further stated that "there was an ethical and moral obligation, and saying it underscored how seriously we took this." However, the Bush administration's recent idea of sending several hundred NATO advisors to support African Union peacekeepers falls short of what many advocates have hoped for.

Facilitator: Thank you so much Emily for being with us today and for sharing with us your views on the conflict in Darfur. You have helped us understand the complexity of the situation and to uncover some of the myths about this terrible war. Whether or not we label the war in Darfur "genocide" or something else, the fact is that the situation is getting worse, and there appears to be no immediate way to improve it.

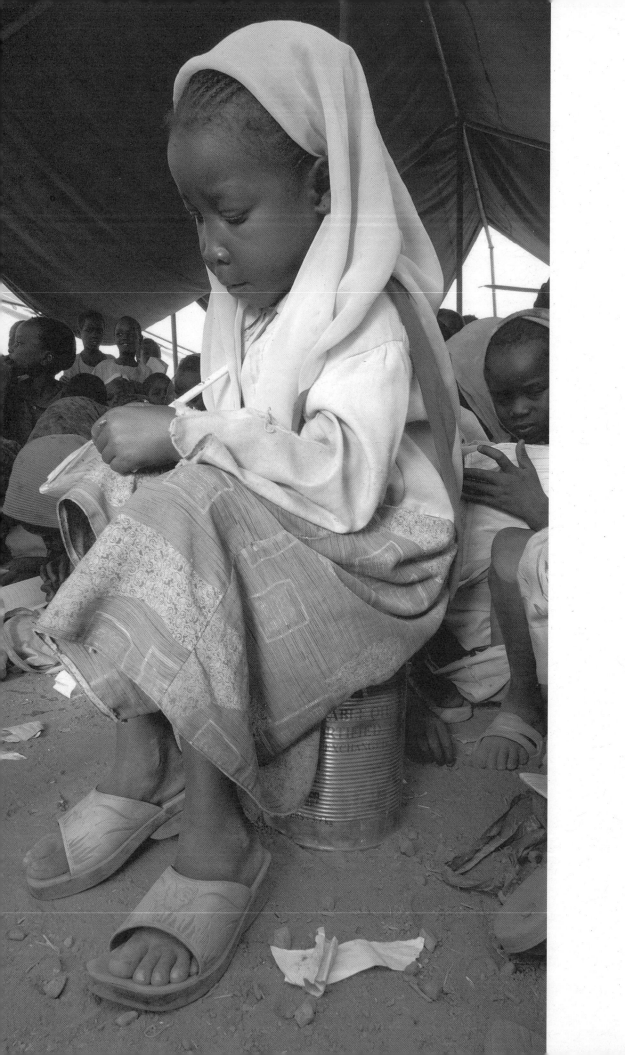

About the Authors

Linda Beher

Telling organizational stories is a favorite role of Linda Beher, who from 2003-2007 was executive secretary, communication and promotions, for United Methodist Committee on Relief, the humanitarian aid and development arm of The United Methodist Church. She reported from some of the world's hot spots during that time: Louisiana and Mississippi in the US; Tbilisi, Georgia; Tirana, Albania; Sarajevo, Bosnia-Herzegovina; and Lubumbashi, Congo.

Her travels also took her to South Darfur, Sudan, where she experienced firsthand the courage and determination of Sudanese people who wanted peace so they could return home. From South Darfur and Khartoum she filed stories on UMCOR's aid to displaced persons in camps near Ed Daein. Along with others in the UMCOR delegation she met with government and humanitarian officials in Khartoum. An accomplished presenter, she has spoken about Sudan's complicated braid of issues before faith communities in Connecticut, New York, and Washington State.

Prior to UMCOR, Ms. Beher worked as a marketing director for Hartford Financial Services Group. Currently she is marketing associate at NetMark, a management consulting practice in Hartford, Connecticut. Educated at McPherson College and Hartford Seminary, she is a member of Asylum Hill Congregational Church, Hartford, and published *The Years We Carry*, a collection of poems, in 2001.

Maxine West

Born in Greensboro, North Carolina, Maxine attended Bennett College, and received a Bachelor of Science degree in mathematics. She taught math and chemistry at Allen High School, Asheville, North Carolina, from 1963 until 1970, and was employed as a research chemist in the Asheville area for fifteen years before joining the executive staff of the Women's Division, General Board of Global Ministries, The United Methodist Church, in 1985.

As staff of the Women's Division, Maxine held the position of executive secretary for organizational development from December 1985 until April 1991. In April 1991, she was elected assistant general secretary for resource management and marketing, with administrative responsibility for the Service Center and *Response* magazine. After nearly 18 years of employment with the Women Division, she retired June 30, 2003.

A frequent contributor to *Response*, Maxine enjoys writing and researching the history of United Methodist Women and the predecessor organizations. She has taught in regional and conference Schools of Christian Mission and is the author of the 2004 study guide for *Concerning Prayer*.

Additional Resources

Map & Facts: Sudan. *By Linda Beher.* This beautiful four-color map, 36" x 23" (folds to 6" x 9") shows topography and major cities in Sudan, in relation to other African countries. Panels on the reverse side provide a ready reference to history, current statistics, religion, mission projects, and basic geographic facts for Sudan.

(M3065-2009-01) $12.00

The Sudan Project: Rebuilding with the People of Darfur, A Young Person's Guide. *By Melissa Leembruggen.* The book, organized around the alphabet, introduces children to Sudan.

(M3056-2009-01) $8.00

Piece Work / Peace Work: Working Together for Peace and Sudan. *By Martha Bettis Gee. Teacher's Guide for Children's Mission Study.* The *Guide* is designed for elementary children from Grades 1-6. The author, using the image of a quilt, asks the children to design their own quilt, while they at the same time learn about the diversity of peoples, traditions, and religious practice in the largest country in Africa. Children will hear about current United Methodist projects, and see how they can respond as Christians to make a difference for the children of Sudan.

(M3063-2009-01) $8.00

Korean Sudan Summary Insert. A synopsis of the Sudan adult mission study written for the Korean edition of the *Interpreter* magazine.

(M5032-2009-01) Free

Spanish Sudan Summary Insert. A synopsis of the Sudan adult mission study written for the Spanish edition of *el Intérprete* magazine.

(M5030-2009-01) Free

When Freedom?/Sudan in Captivity. This DVD was produced by Friendship Press.

(M3064-2009-01) $19.95

Response magazine, April 2009

(R3023-2009-01) $2.75

New World Outlook magazine, May-June 2009

(NW3003-2009-01) $3.00

Website: http://new.gbgm-umc.org/umw/sudan